Practical Piano Illustrated

Keys, Scales, Chords and
Theory for Beginners

By

Austin Middleton

Dedicated to Suzanne, Juvenal Middleton

1925-2010

Practical Piano Illustrated

Table of Contents

I. HOW TO USE THIS BOOK

This book is meant to serve as an introduction to the piano for the person who is just beginning his or her journey on the keyboard. Many people do not have easy or affordable access to a piano instructor but are still anxious to learn to play. How, then, to get started? Where should a new student begin? What topics should be studied first? Where can a student find accurate information that is needed to begin? These are fundamental questions which a beginning student will likely be asking. In response to these queries, I have attempted to present practical and useful information in such a way that the new student can immediately begin to play while, at the same time, introducing the student to the basics of practical music theory.

This book was written with one purpose in mind, that is, to get the new student playing as soon as possible. I have attempted to cover the main topics at a fundamental level. Further in-depth study will be required, of course, but this book will allow a new student to begin to play right away. I have attempted to add new concepts and new topics in a logical progression to encourage growth and development.

For example, a student may not completely understand what is meant when we say that a piece of music is in a certain key. Without going into a lot of technical detail, but by following the keyboard diagrams, the student can immediately begin to play scales in each key. What is unique about this book is that the scales for each key are clearly denoted on the keyboard diagrams. The patterns are easily memorized (granted, some more easily than others) and combined with a gradual introduction to basic music theory regarding intervals, a working familiarity of keys will be achieved.

I have laid out in easy to follow format the scales in the major keys, the scales in the natural minor keys and the blues scales. Again, the emphasis is on the student starting to play; for example, if the student starts to play the blues scale, up and down the keyboard, he or she will hear the distinctive sound of the blues and will appreciate the unique emotional pull of that sound. The blues are a unique and distinct style of music, and a basic exposure to the blues will bring immeasurable pleasure to the student who begins to explore the genre.

Once a student becomes familiar with the scales in each key, then playing chords in those keys would be the logical next step. After learning the ins and outs of playing chords in each key, the student will begin to understand chord progressions, that is, the natural flow of chords which follow each other, often building tension and then resolving themselves musically. An ideal vehicle, or technique for working with the idea of chord progressions, tension and resolution is the 12 Bar Blues. At first, the student may not realize that he or she has just unlocked a major treasure trove-but again, taking the ideas presented in the following pages and trying them out on the keyboard, the student will quickly recognize the pattern and the potential of this arrangement.

The student is take these ideas one or two at a time, and experiment and find their own sound.

Throughout the text, you will find sections entitled **Side Notes**, **Test Your Understanding** and occasionally a **Quick Quiz**. These allow the reader to step back for a moment, think about what we are learning, and then apply the knowledge in a practical way.

One final brief word, because I know you want to get on with it and not listen to some long- winded philosophy. One final word......as you start to read through this book, you may encounter words or concepts that you do not immediately understand. Don't worry about it....skip that part, keep reading, keep trying to put the pieces together and before you know it things will start to fall into place. For example, when you first encounter the idea of "intervals" you may not get it at first. Don't sweat it, my brother or sister. Skip that part for now; play some scales, play some chords, don't throw the book down and say that it makes no sense. Skip that part and believe me, as your brain starts to put together all this new information, someday soon, you will suddenly get it and when you do, you are on your way to great joy and great satisfaction. What seems difficult today will, in a short time, become second nature and you will soon start "jazzing it up". I say go for it. Show them what you can do. God has given you an imagination and all kinds of creativity. Exercise it, use it, be unafraid on your musical journey.

Believe me, I want each one of you to find peace, joy and fulfillment in your soul as you lose yourself in the sound and the joy of the keyboard.

Best wishes to every one of you,

Blake Middleton

II. SCALE PATTERNS AND KEYBOARD DIAGRAMS
MAJOR SCALES

The keyboard diagrams on the following pages will allow you to quickly begin to play and to visualize how the notes relate to each other. You will likely refer back to the keyboard diagrams throughout your studies. Personally, I am a very visual type of learner. If I can see a diagram or drawing, I am then able to absorb and retain that information much better than if I had simply read about it or heard somebody try to explain it.

Study the patterns on these scales. The round dots on the piano keys indicate which notes belong to that key. <u>All dots belong in the key; the red ones are linked together in an octave, while the blues ones are in the same key but a different octave. Don't let the color coding throw you off.</u> The lines connecting the dots create a pattern, or shape. Many of these shapes will immediately, and readily, be impressed upon your memory. You will also notice that the lines are different colors (like the dots mentioned above).   This is merely to help you visualize the notes in each octave.

One of my favorites, to use as an example, is the key of ***Eb major*** (pronounced E flat major). Let's look at the layout of the ***Eb major*** scale.

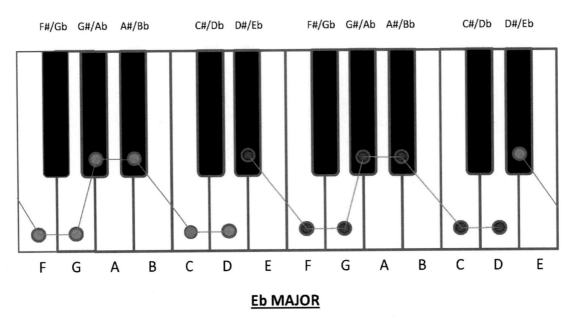

Eb MAJOR

Starting at Eb (which we call the _tonic_, or first note of the Eb scale), we see two notes "down" (F and G) then two notes "up" (Ab and Bb), then two notes "down" (C and D) then back to Eb. I know this description sounds rather unsophisticated, but this is an easy way to visualize and learn all the notes which make up the key of ***Eb major***. Of course, you can continue going up the keyboard, playing the scale of ***Eb major***, going higher and higher, one octave at a time.

Take it one key signature at a time. You do not need to learn all the keys in one day. Some keys you will enjoy more than others. Some are naturally easier to play, some are easier to memorize, some may have a certain sound that you like. This is your musical journey, so learn, experiment and, most of all, play. In time it will become second nature to you to be able to move up and down the keyboard playing scales in every key.

Once you start to really know which notes make up a key, you will start to see a pattern emerging. We will learn later about the ***Whole-Whole-Half-Whole-Whole-Whole-Half*** pattern that is used to create a major scale. All major scales use this pattern; in fact, this pattern is the definition of a major scale.

> **Side note:** The Whole-Whole-Half-Whole-Whole-Whole-Half pattern is really a *sequence of intervals*. What is an *interval*? An interval is quite simply the distance between any two notes on the keyboard.
> When we say, "Whole", we mean <u>two</u> semi-tones. One semi-tone is one key on the piano. So, a "Whole" is two semi-tones, or two piano keys.
> When we say "Half", we mean <u>one</u> semi-tone, or one piano key. One semi-tone equals one piano key, which means that a step of one semi-tone takes you to the piano key immediately adjacent. Immediately adjacent means just that, regardless if that piano key is white (whole notes) or black (sharps and flats).

Let's go back to our keyboard diagram of ***Eb major***. Starting at Eb, what is the next note in that key? It is F.

What is the interval between Eb and F? It is a "step" of two piano keys, or two semi-tones, or what we call a "Whole". What is the next note in the key of Eb? It is G. What is the interval, or distance, between F and G? It is also two piano keys, or two semi-tones, or what we call "Whole".
Did you forget to count the black key (Gb) which is between F and G? When we are counting intervals, we need to count all keys, not just the white keys. Continuing this sequence of intervals, we can then derive, or calculate, which notes make up the key of Eb major, or any other major key. Study this concept and become familiar with the idea of intervals. We will be using the concept of intervals more and more. An understanding of intervals is critical as we move into chords and beyond.

Before we dive into the keyboard diagrams, let's regroup a minute and think about what we are doing. Keep the following points in mind as you study the keyboard diagrams;

1. The key is given in upper right of page. The letter and flat or sharp that is indicated in the upper corner of the page is the key's *identity*. Whether it is major or minor is known as it's *quality*.

2. The notes that are included in the scale have been calculated, or laid out, by following the templates that we discussed earlier. Starting at the tonic, or first note of the key that we are in, we build the scale using these templates.

    Major scales   W W H W W W H
    Minor scales   W H W W H W W

3. Remember that a W means Whole. A Whole is two semi-tones, or two piano keys. An H means Half, and that is one semi-tone, or one piano key.

4. The notes of the scale are identified by roman numerals. You will see some roman numerals are upper case, and some are lower case. For now, don't worry about that; we will cover all that when we get into major and minor chords.

5. Speaking of chords—you can quickly learn to play chords using these keyboard diagrams. Play the three notes together.

    Play the first, third and fifth note of the major scale you are in. (I, iii, V)
    Play the second, fourth and sixth note (ii, IV, vi)
    Play the third, fifth and seventh notes (iii, V, vii)
    You see how we are playing every other note.

Of course, later on, we will be playing much more complex chords, but for now, enjoy the sounds of the chords. If we are playing the chords in root position, the identity of the chord will be the lowest note. Later we will learn about chord inversions where we play the same tones, but in a different order. Don't worry, we will get around to that.

<u>**Test your understanding**</u>: One of your musician friends stops by and says to you, "Let's play a one-four-five in <u>G</u>." What does he mean by this?

Let's discuss: First of all, since he said, "G", that means G major. Unless someone specifically says the term "minor", or other modifier, we can assume that "major" is intended.

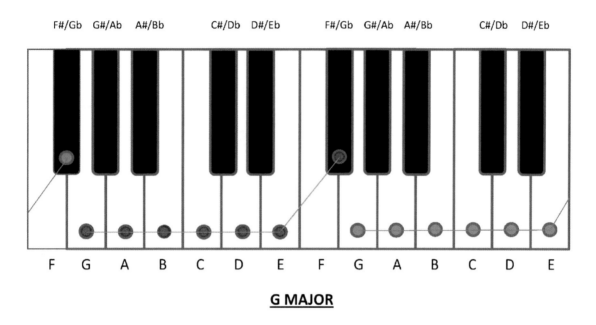

G MAJOR

Now, about that one-four-five: Let's look at the keyboard diagram for G. We see the I, IV and V (pronounced "one, four and five") notes of that scale, listed as below;

I	ii	iii	IV	V	vi	vii	I
G	A	B	C	D	E	F#	G

   G is the first, or I, note in the key of G.
     C is the fourth, or IV, note in the key of G.
       D is the fifth, or V, note in the key of G.

Okay, we now understand that we will be playing a sequence of chords. Playing chords by themselves is great but linking them in a sequence is even better. Playing chords in certain patterns is called "chord progression" and we will learn more about that later in this book. But for now, follow your friends lead and play a I-IV-V (pronounced one-four-five), playing each chord cleanly and clearly, then moving to the next chord.

Your friend may very well be leading you into the 12 bar blues, and that is a very good thing. Much more about the 12-bar blues in Chapter VIII.

Degree	Chord	Notes	
I	G	G B D	(I, iii, V)
IV	C	C E G	(IV, vi, I)
V:	D	D F# A	(V, vii, ii)

Quick Quiz: We just played three chords; a <u>G chord</u>, a <u>C chord</u> and a <u>D chord</u>, all in the key of G major, or G.

Each chord was made up of three notes. When we play a <u>D chord</u>, for example, we are playing **D, F#** and **A.**

Why do these three notes create a D <u>major</u> chord?

If we wanted to, how would we quickly change to a D <u>minor</u> chord?

Let's discuss: To answer these questions, let's go to the keyboard. Let's examine the <u>D major chord</u> and look at the interval, or distance between the first note (D) of the chord and the middle note (F#) of the chord. Let's count the semi-tones....

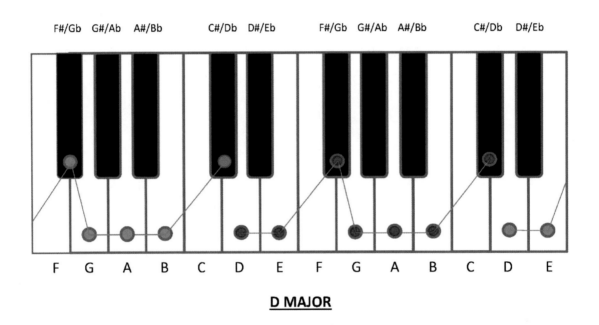

D MAJOR

Starting at D, one semi-tone to D#, second semi-tone to E, third semi-tone to F, and finally a fourth semi-tone to F#, the middle note of the chord. This is an interval of <u>4 semi-tones</u>. An interval of 4 semi-tones between the first and middle notes of a triad chord is the definition of a major chord.

Now, suppose we played the notes D, F and A. In other words, we are "flattening" the second note, thereby decreasing the interval between the first and middle note. Now what is the interval between the first note (D) and the middle note (F)?

Counting as we did before, starting at D, one semi-tone to D#, second semi-tone to E and third semi-tone to F. This interval of <u>three semi-tones</u> between the first and middle note of a chord is the definition of what makes a minor chord.

We will discuss intervals in more detail later in Chapter VI.

Key: **A Major**

I	ii	iii	IV	V	vi	vii	I
A	B	C#	D	E	F#	G#	A

Degree	Chord	Notes		
I:	A	A	C#	E
ii:	Bm	B	D	F#
iii:	C#m	C#	E	G#
IV:	D	D	F#	A
V:	E	E	G#	B
vi:	F#m	F#	A	C#
vii:	G# dim	G#	B	D

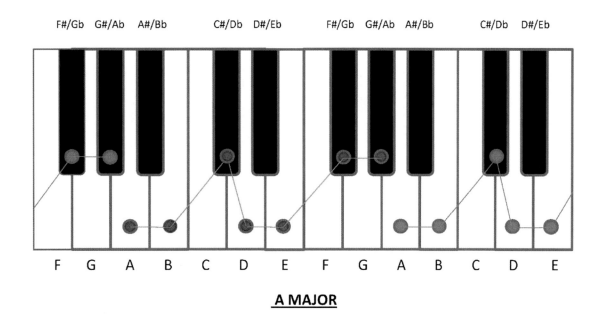

A MAJOR

I	ii	iii	IV	V	vi	vii	I
Ab	Bb	C	Db	Eb	F	G	Ab

Degree	Chord	Notes		
I:	Ab	Ab	C	Eb
ii:	Bbm	Bb	Db	F
iii:	Cm	C	Eb	G
IV:	Db	Db	F	Ab
V:	Eb	Eb	G	Bb
vi:	Fm	F	Ab	C
vii:	G dim	G	Bb	Db

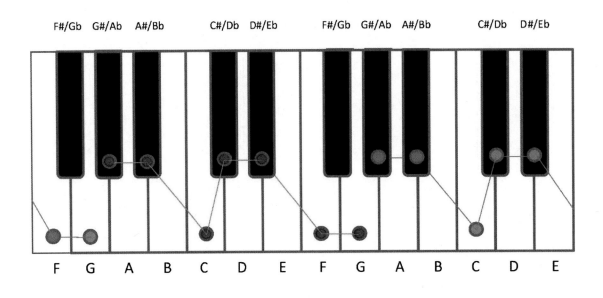

Ab MAJOR

Key: B Major

I	ii	iii	IV	V	vi	vii	I
B	C#	D#	E	F#	G#	A#	B

Degree	Chord	Notes
I:	B	B D# F#
ii:	C#m	C# E G#
iii:	D#m	D# F# A#
IV:	E	E G# B
V:	F#	F# A# C#
vi:	G#m	G# B D#
vii:	Bb dim	A# C# E

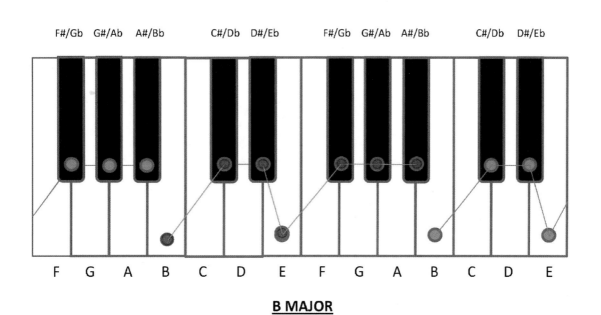

B MAJOR

Key: **Bb Major**

I	ii	iii	IV	V	vi	vii	I
Bb	C	D	Eb	F	G	A	Bb

Degree	Chord	Notes		
I:	Bb	Bb	D	F
ii:	Cm	C	Eb	G
iii:	Dm	D	F	A
IV:	Eb	Eb	G	Bb
V:	F	F	A	C
vi:	Gm	G	Bb	D
vii:	A dim	A	C	Eb

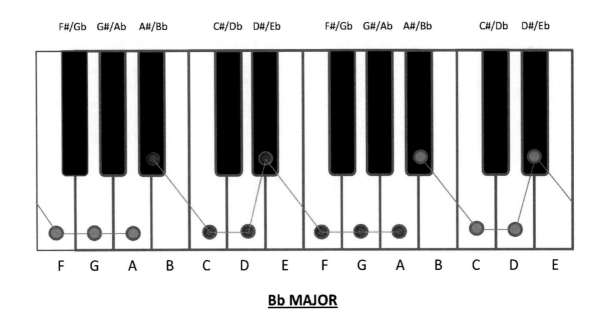

Bb MAJOR

I	ii	iii	IV	V	vi	vii	I
C	D	E	F	G	A	B	C

Degree	Chord	Notes		
I:	C	C	E	G
ii:	Dm	D	F	A
iii:	Em	E	G	B
IV:	F	F	A	C
V:	G	G	B	D
vi:	Am	A	C	E
vii:	B dim	B	D	F

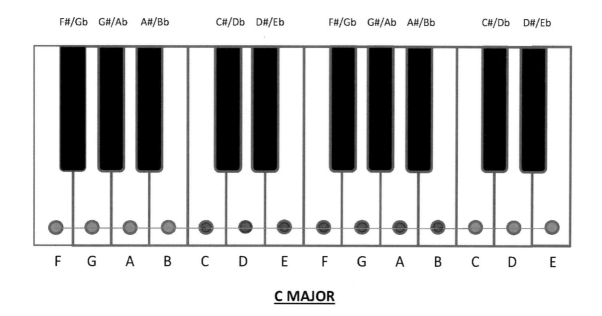

C MAJOR

I	ii	iii	IV	V	vi	vii	I
C#	D#	F	F#	G#	A#	C	C#

Degree	Chord	Notes		
I:	C#	C#	F	G#
ii:	Ebm	D#	F#	A#
iii:	Fm	F	G#	C
IV:	F#	F#	A#	C#
V:	G#	G#	C	D#
vi:	Bbm	A#	C#	F
vii:	C dim	C	D#	F#

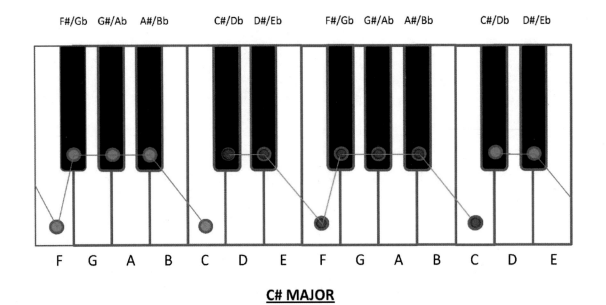

C# MAJOR

Key: **D Major**

I	ii	iii	IV	V	vi	vii	I
D	E	F#	G	A	B	C#	D

Degree	Chord	Notes		
I:	D	D	F#	A
ii:	Em	E	G	B
iii:	F#m	F#	A	C#
IV:	G	G	B	D
V:	A	A	C#	E
vi:	Bm	B	D	F#
vii:	C# dim	C#	E	G

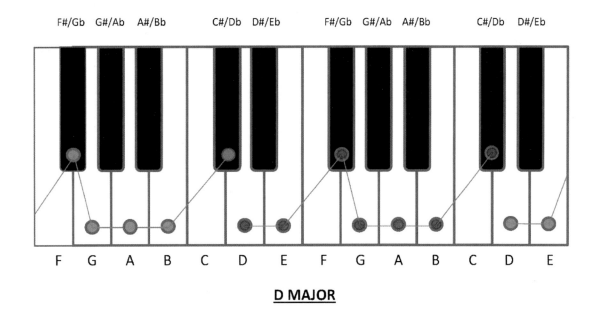

D MAJOR

Key: **E Major**

I	ii	iii	IV	V	vi	vii	I
E	F#	G#	A	B	C#	D#	E

Degree	Chord	Notes		
I:	E	E	G#	B
ii:	F#m	F#	A	C#
iii:	G#m	G#	B	D#
IV:	A	A	C#	E
V:	B	B	D#	F#
vi:	C#m	C#	E	G#
vii:	D# dim	D#	F#	A

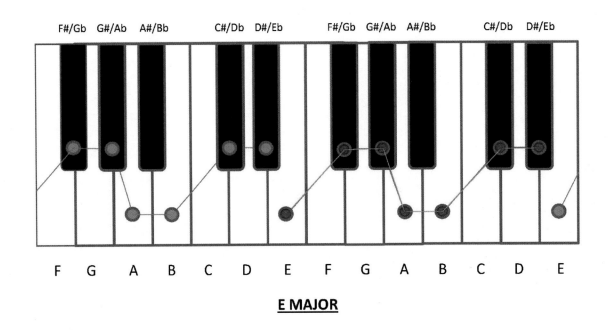

E MAJOR

Key: **Eb Major**

I	ii	iii	IV	V	vi	vii	I
Eb	F	G	Ab	Bb	C	D	Eb

Degree	Chord	Notes		
I:	Eb	Eb	G	Bb
ii:	Fm	F	Ab	C
iii:	Gm	G	Bb	D
IV:	Ab	Ab	C	Eb
V:	Bb	Bb	D	F
vi:	Cm	C	Eb	G
vii:	D dim	D	F	Ab

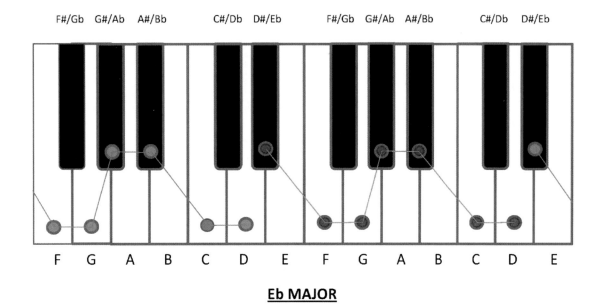

Eb MAJOR

I	ii	iii	IV	V	vi	vii	I
F	G	A	Bb	C	D	E	F

Degree	Chord	Notes		
I:	F	F	A	C
ii:	Gm	G	Bb	D
iii:	Am	A	C	E
IV:	Bb	Bb	D	F
V:	C	C	E	G
vi:	Dm	D	F	A
vii:	E dim	E	G	Bb

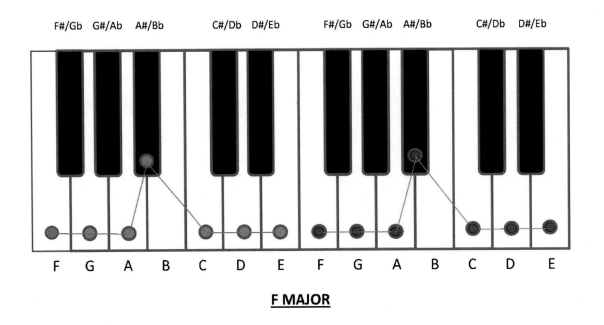

F MAJOR

Key: **G Major**

I	ii	iii	IV	V	vi	vii	I
G	A	B	C	D	E	F#	G

Degree	**Chord**	**Notes**		
I:	G	G	B	D
ii:	Am	A	C	E
iii:	Bm	B	D	F#
IV:	C	C	E	G
V:	D	D	F#	A
vi:	Em	E	G	B
vii:	F# dim	F#	A	C

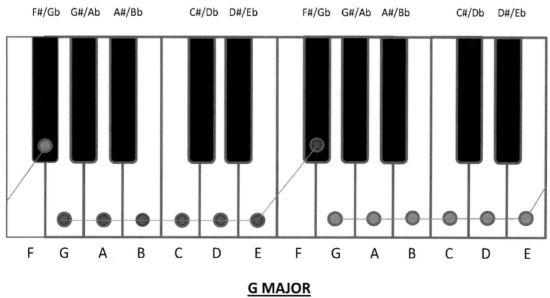

G MAJOR

I	ii	iii	IV	V	vi	vii	I
Gb	Ab	Bb	B	Db	Eb	F	Gb

Degree	**Chord**	**Notes**		
I:	Gb	Gb	Bb	Db
ii:	Abm	Ab	B	Eb
iii:	Bbm	Bb	Db	F
IV:	B	B	Eb	Gb
V:	Db	Db	F	Ab
vi:	Ebm	Eb	Gb	Bb
vii:	F dim	F	Ab	B

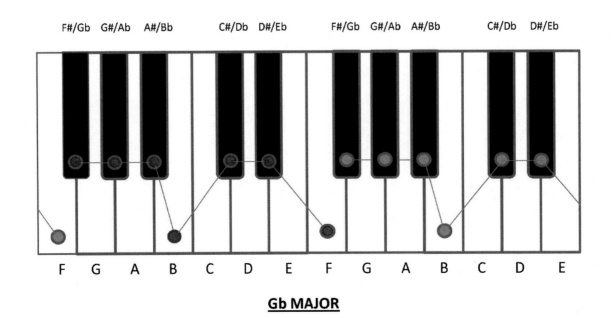

Gb MAJOR

III. SCALE PATTERNS AND KEYBOARD DIAGRAMS
MINOR SCALES

The keyboard diagrams on the following pages will allow you to quickly begin to play and to visualize how the notes relate to each other. As you begin to move up and down the keyboard, getting familiar with the minor scales, I think that you will agree that the minor scales have a distinctive sound in which even a simple melody can evoke emotions and complex feelings. That is one of the joys of playing in the minor scales.

Look at the patterns on these scales. The round dots on the piano keys indicate which notes belong to that key. All dots belong in the key; the red ones are linked together in an octave, while the blues ones are in the same key but a different octave. Don't let the color coding throw you off. The lines connecting the dots create a pattern, or shape. Many of these shapes will immediately, and readily, be impressed upon your memory.

For an example, let's examine the notes, and the corresponding pattern, which make up the key of **Eb minor**. This is a beautiful key and very easy to learn. Starting on **Eb**, the root note, we move diagonally to **F**, then three black keys in succession (**Gb, Ab, Bb**), drop almost straight down to **B**. See how this **B** note almost "mirrors" the **F** note played previously. In other words, the three black keys (**Gb, Ab, Bb**) are "bracketed" by **F** and **B**. That is 5 notes out of the 7 you need to memorize. Add the other two black keys (**Db** and **Eb**) and you have just memorized the **Eb minor** scale.

I must make something clear to the student at this point. We are in the process of learning what is known as the "natural" minor scale. There are other minor scales (harmonic minor, melodic minor, pentatonic, and others.) In time, your studies will take you there; but for now, the natural minor scale is what we are focusing on. We are building a foundation here and, in time, you will surely be playing in all the minor scales.

RELATIVE SCALES

While we are exploring the minor scales, let's discuss something called a relative scale. Without going too deeply into the how and why, let's examine the keyboard diagram for **C major** and compare that to the keyboard diagram for **A minor**. We see that both scales (and therefore, both keys) are made up of the same notes although the root notes are, of course, different. We can say that **A minor** is the relative minor of **C major**. We can also say that **C major** is the relative major of **A minor**.

Let's look at another example. If we examine the keyboard diagram for **Db major** and compare the notes in that scale to the keyboard diagram of **Bb minor**, we find a similar situation. The notes that make up each scale are identical, but of course they are in a different order because they start on a different root note. In this example, we can say that **Bb minor** is the relative minor of **Db major**. Conversely, we can say that **Db major** is the relative major of **Bb minor**.

Relative major key	Relative minor key
Ab major	F minor
A major	Gb minor
Bb major	G minor
B major	Ab minor
C major	A minor
Db major	Bb minor
D major	B minor
Eb major	C minor
E major	Db minor
F major	D minor
Gb major	Eb minor
G major	E minor

If you study the above chart you will see that a relative minor key is three semi-tones below it's corresponding major key.

For example, look at a major key......let us pick **Bb major**. On the keyboard, move down three semi-tones (which we know by now are three piano keys). Where do we end up? We end up on G. G minor is the relative minor of Bb major.

Pick another example......pick a minor key.........Db minor......move up 3 semi-tones and we land on E. Therefore, Db minor is the relative minor of E major.

Without losing too much sleep over this, we need to think about why this is happening.

Back when we were first learning about how a scale is produced; that is, the pattern of intervals which gave each scale a structure. Remember the major scale had its own template and the minor scale had its own template. This is what we had discussed back then:

Major scales   W W H W W W H
Minor scales   W H W W H W W

We mentioned that the minor relative scale is three semi-tones lower than its major relative scale. The other thing we know is that all the notes are the same in both relative scales. Let's try something here to try to understand this.

Suppose we slide the minor scale template 3 semi-tones to the left. It would look like this. Comparing the scale of Bb major and the scale of G minor is shown here:

Major scale   **Bb** w **C** w **D** H **Eb** w **F** w **G** w **A** H **Bb**
Minor scale   **G** w **A** H **Bb** w **C** w **D** H **Eb** w **F** w **G**

 I know this is a little abstract, and maybe wasn't on our agenda to think about this particular topic, but we have been talking about intervals. All we are doing here is taking two templates, and then sliding one to the left three semi-tones, and now we see why the notes of a major relative key are identical to the notes of a minor key which is three semi-tones lower.

For now, study the keyboard diagrams for the minor scales. Listen for their unique, emotional sounds. Experiment with playing chord with your left hand and playing very simple, short melodies with your right. You will very soon be putting together short pieces that contain a short melody of 5 or 6 notes, accentuated by some moody, or emotional chords. Experiment, play and enjoy; you will find that the minor scales have their own beautiful appeal.

Key: **A minor**

$\underline{i}$	$\underline{ii}$	$\underline{III}$	$\underline{iv}$	$\underline{v}$	$\underline{VI}$	$\underline{VI}$	$\underline{i}$
A	B	C	D	E	F	G	A

Degree	**Chord**	**Notes**		
i:	Am	A	C	E
ii:	Bdim	B	D	F
III:	C	C	E	G
iv:	Dm	D	F	A
v:	Em	E	G	B
VI:	F	F	A	C
VII:	G	G	B	D

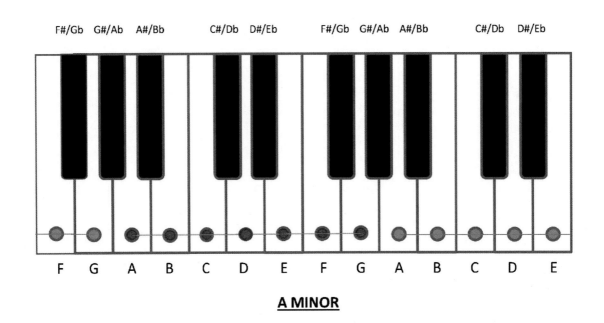

A MINOR

Key: **Ab minor**

i	ii	III	iv	v	VI	VII	i
Ab	Bb	B	Db	Eb	E	Gb	Ab

Degree	**Chord**	**Notes**		
i:	Abm	Ab	B	Eb
ii:	Bbdim	Bb	Db	E
III:	B	B	Eb	Gb
iv:	Dbm	Db	E	Ab
v:	Ebm	Eb	Gb	Bb
VI:	E	E	Ab	B
VII:	Gb	Gb	Bb	Db

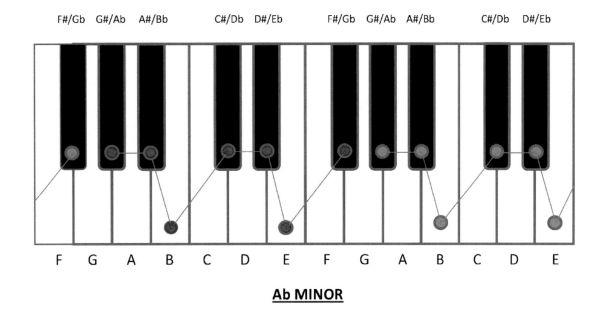

Ab MINOR

Key: **B minor**

i	ii	III	iv	v	VI	VII	i
B	C#	D	E	F#	G	A	B

Degree	Chord	Notes		
i:	Bm	B	D	F#
ii:	C#dim	C#	E	G
III:	D	D	F#	A
iv:	Em	E	G	B
v:	F#m	F#	A	C#
VI:	G	G	B	D
VII:	A	A	C#	E

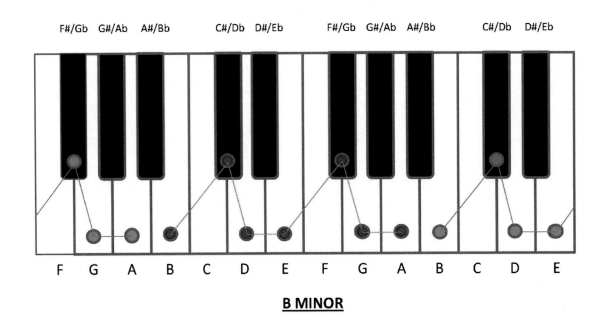

B MINOR

i	ii	III	iv	v	VI	VII	i
Bb	C	Db	Eb	F	Gb	Ab	Bb

Degree	**Chord**	**Notes**		
i:	Bbm	Bb	Db	F
ii:	Cdim	C	Eb	Gb
III:	Db	Db	F	Ab
iv:	Ebm	Eb	Gb	Bb
v:	Fm	F	Ab	C
VI:	Gb	Gb	Bb	Db
VII:	Ab	Ab	C	Eb

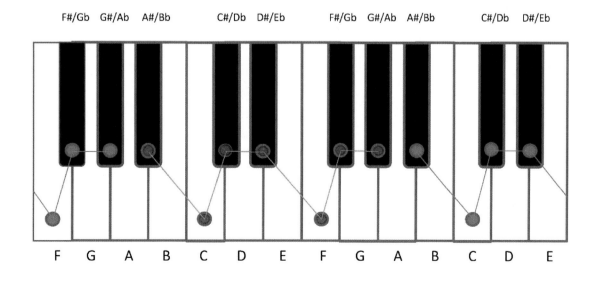

Bb MINOR

Key: **C minor**

$\underline{i}$	$\underline{ii}$	$\underline{III}$	$\underline{iv}$	$\underline{v}$	$\underline{VI}$	$\underline{VII}$	$\underline{i}$
C	D	D#	F	G	G#	A#	C

Degree	**Chord**	**Notes**		
i:	Cm	C	D#	G
ii:	Ddim	D	F	G#
III:	D#	D#	G	A#
iv:	Fm	F	G#	C
v:	Gm	G	A#	D
VI:	Ab	G#	C	D#
VII:	Bb	A#	D	F

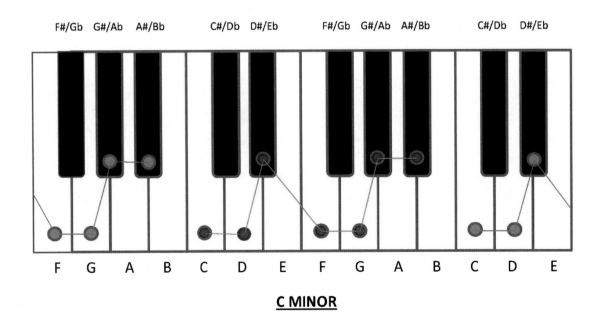

C MINOR

Key: **D minor**

i	ii	III	iv	v	VI	VII	i
D	E	F	G	A	A#	C	D

Degree	Chord	Notes		
i:	Dm	D	F	A
ii:	Edim	E	G	A#
III:	F	F	A	C
iv:	Gm	G	A#	D
v:	Am	A	C	E
VI:	Bb	A#	D	F
VII:	C	C	E	G

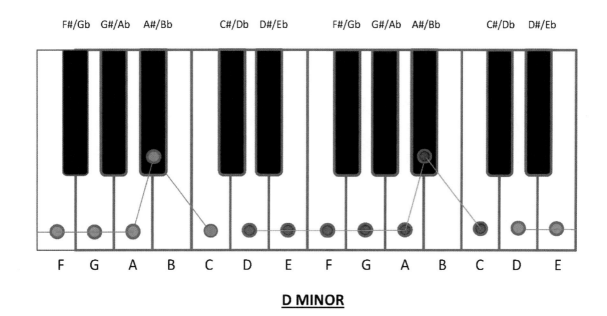

D MINOR

i	ii	III	iv	v	VI	VII	i
Db	Eb	E	Gb	Ab	A	B	Db

Degree	Chord	Notes		
i:	Dbm	Db	E	Ab
ii:	Eb dim	Eb	Gb	A
III:	E	E	Ab	B
iv:	Gbm	Gb	A	Db
v:	Abm	Ab	B	Eb
VI:	A	A	Db	E
VII:	B	B	Eb	Gb

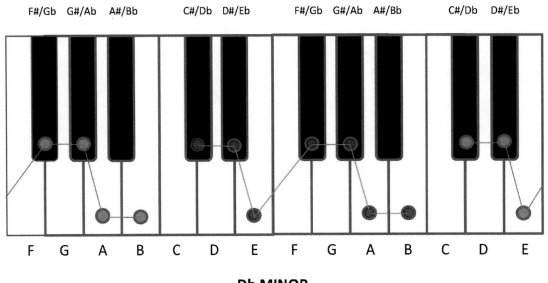

Db MINOR

i	ii	III	iv	v	VI	VII	i
E	F#	G	A	B	C	D	E

Degree	Chord	Notes		
i:	Em	E	G	B
ii:	F# dim	F#	A	C
III:	G	G	B	D
iv:	Am	A	C	E
v:	Bm	B	D	F#
VI:	C	C	E	G
VII:	D	D	F#	A

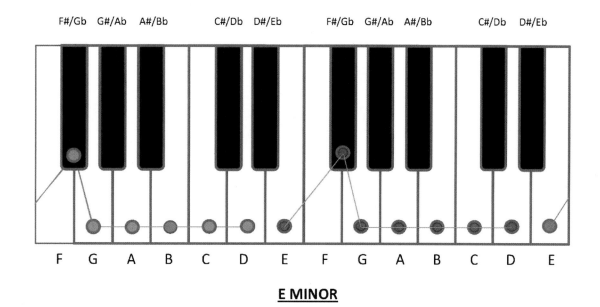

E MINOR

Key: **Eb minor**

i	ii	III	iv	v	VI	VII	i
Eb	F	Gb	Ab	Bb	B	Db	Eb

Degree	**Chord**	**Notes**		
i:	Ebm	Eb	Gb	Bb
ii:	F dim	F	Ab	B
III:	Gb	Gb	Bb	Db
iv:	Abm	Ab	B	Eb
v:	Bbm	Bb	Db	F
VI:	B	B	Eb	Gb
VII:	Db	Db	F	Ab

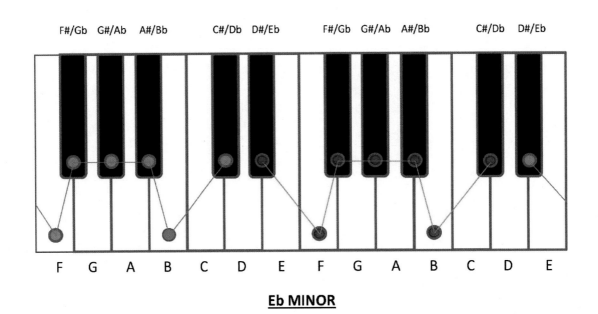

Eb MINOR

Key: **F minor**

<u>i</u>	<u>ii</u>	<u>III</u>	<u>iv</u>	<u>v</u>	<u>VI</u>	<u>VII</u>	<u>i</u>
F	G	Ab	Bb	C	Db	Eb	F

Degree	**Chord**	**Notes**		
i:	Fm	F	Ab	C
ii:	G dim	G	Bb	Db
III:	Ab	Ab	C	Eb
iv:	Bbm	Bb	Db	F
v:	Cm	C	Eb	G
VI:	Db	Db	F	Ab
VII:	Eb	Eb	G	Bb

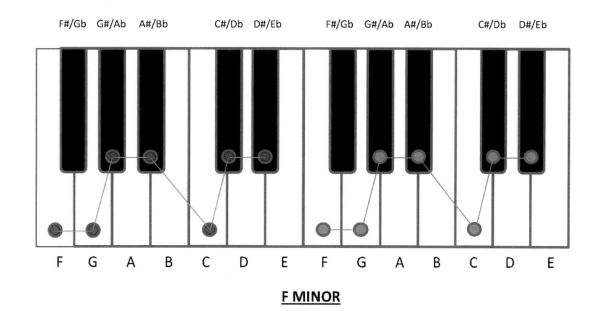

F MINOR

Key: **G minor**

i	ii	III	iv	v	VI	VII	i
G	A	A#	C	D	D#	F	G

Degree	Chord	Notes		
i:	Gm	G	A#	D
ii:	A dim	A	C	D#
III:	Bb	A#	D	F
iv:	Cm	C	D#	G
v:	Dm	D	F	A
VI:	Eb	D#	G	A#
VII:	F	F	A	C

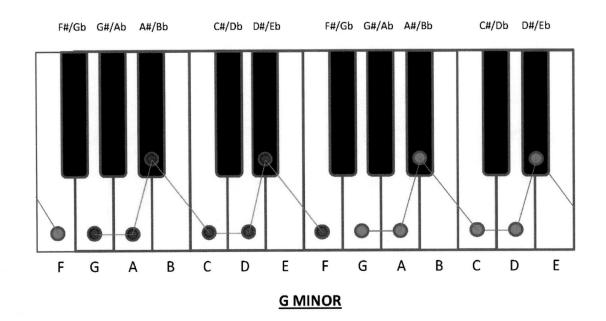

G MINOR

Key: **Gb minor**

i	ii	III	iv	v	VI	VII	i
Gb	Ab	A	B	Db	D	E	Gb

Degree	**Chord**	**Notes**		
i:	Gbm	Gb	A	Db
ii:	Ab dim	Ab	B	D
III:	A	A	Db	E
iv:	Bm	B	D	Gb
v:	Dbm	Db	E	Ab
VI:	D	D	Gb	A
VII:	E	E	Ab	B

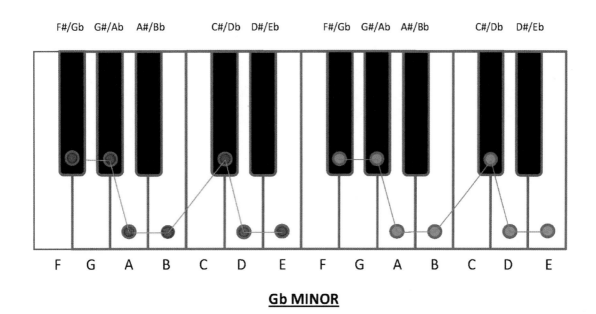

Gb MINOR

IV. SCALE PATTERNS AND KEYBOARD DIAGRAMS
BLUES SCALES

I am somewhat hesitant to open up this "Pandora's Box" of the blues. I love the blues and I know that you will too. But it will take some discipline on your part to keep a balanced approach to your study of the keyboard. Playing the blues is so rewarding and the blues sound is so soulful and sensual that you can easily be distracted from a more well-rounded approach to the keyboard. The blues are an integral part of jazz, improvisation and some would say even gospel. Just once up and down a blues scale on the keyboard and you may very well be inspired to develop a cool bass rhythm in your left hand while your right hand plays a simple melody that takes the listener on an emotional journey.

With that said, let's examine the blues scale and how it is structured.

Let's start with the basic template for the blues scale.
The numbers indicate the number of semi-tones steps to the next note.

3   2   1   1   3   2

For our first example, let's start with the key of Blues in C

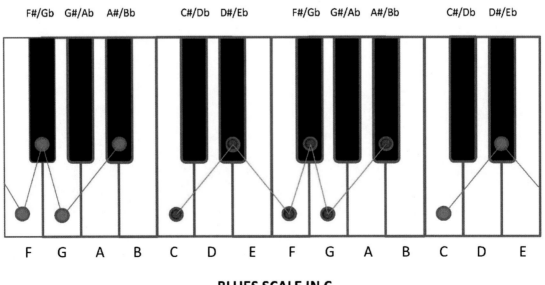

BLUES SCALE IN C

Starting at the root C, go three semi-tones to D#, go 2 semi-tones to F, go 1 semi-tone to F#, go 1 semi-tone to G, go 3 semi-tones to A# and finally go 2 semi-tones and you will land on the root C, one octave higher from where we started. As you play these notes you will immediately hear a distinct blues sound which is similar in all the keys.

	3	2	1	1	3	2	
C	D#	F	F#	G	A#	C	

Let's try another example, this time in key of Bb Blues

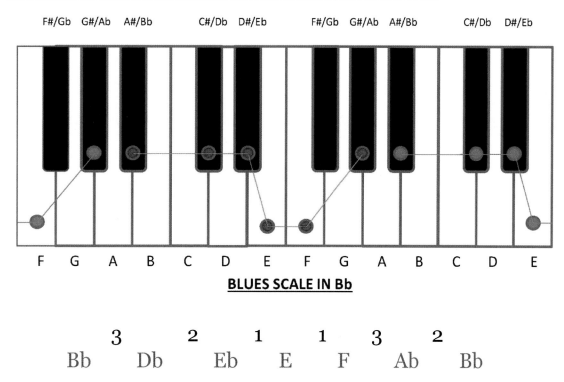

BLUES SCALE IN Bb

	3	2	1	1	3	2
Bb	Db	Eb	E	F	Ab	Bb

Starting on any note, move through the intervals as shown above and you will start to get the sense of the blues scale. One of the distinctive characteristics of the blues scale is that the 3rd, 4th, and 5th notes are all right next to each other. There is one semi-tone between notes 3 and 4 and 1 semi-tone between notes 4 and 5. This gives the scale an incredible range of emotions as the note you are expecting to resolve the tension, just misses, perhaps, opening up another whole range of possible melodies.

Blues Scale in A

I	II	III	IV	V	VI	I
A	C	D	D#	E	G	A

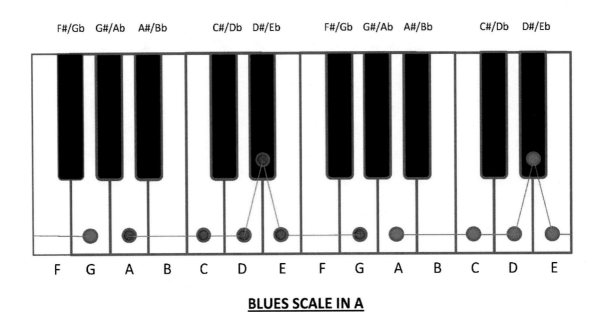

BLUES SCALE IN A

Blues Scale in Ab

I	II	III	IV	V	VI	I
Ab	B	C#	D	Eb	Gb	Ab

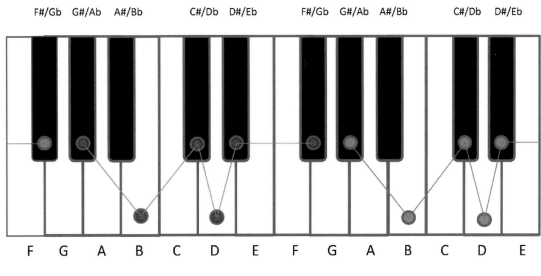

BLUES SCALE IN Ab

Blues Scale in B

$\underline{I}$	$\underline{II}$	$\underline{III}$	$\underline{IV}$	$\underline{V}$	$\underline{VI}$	$\underline{I}$
B	D	E	F	F#	A	B

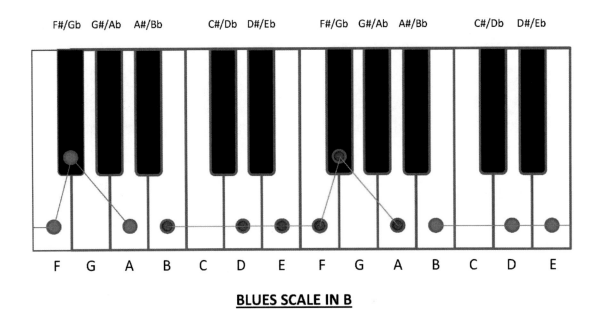

BLUES SCALE IN B

Blues Scale in Bb

$\underline{\text{I}}$	$\underline{\text{II}}$	$\underline{\text{III}}$	$\underline{\text{IV}}$	$\underline{\text{V}}$	$\underline{\text{VI}}$	$\underline{\text{I}}$
Bb	Db	Eb	E	F	Ab	Bb

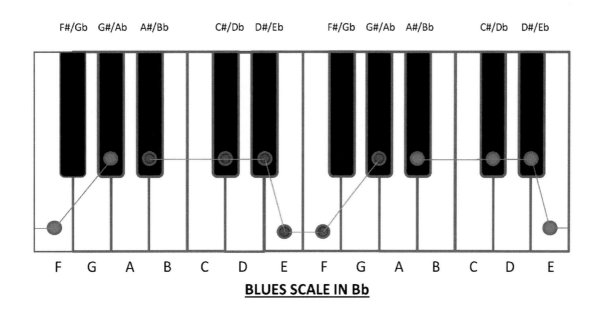

BLUES SCALE IN Bb

Blues Scale in C

I	II	III	IV	V	VI	I
C	Eb	F	F#	G	Bb	C

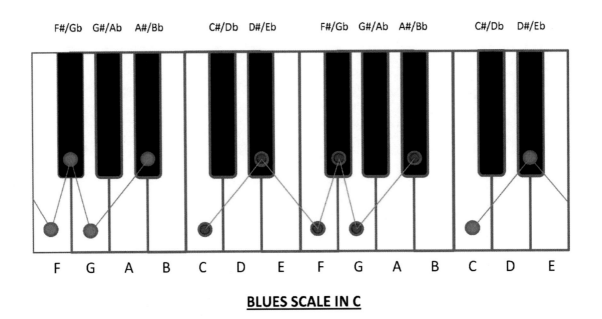

BLUES SCALE IN C

Blues Scale in D

I	II	III	IV	V	VI	I
D	F	G	G#	A	C	D

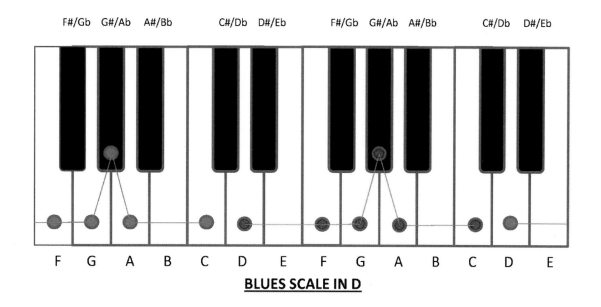

BLUES SCALE IN D

Blues Scale in Db

I	II	III	IV	V	VI	I
Db	D#	E	F	G#	A#	Db

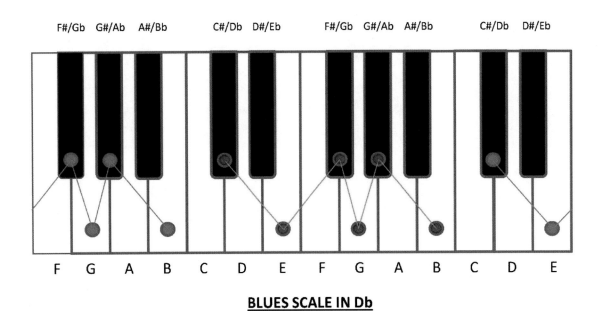

BLUES SCALE IN Db

Blues Scale in E

I	II	III	IV	V	VI	I
E	G	A	A#	B	D	E

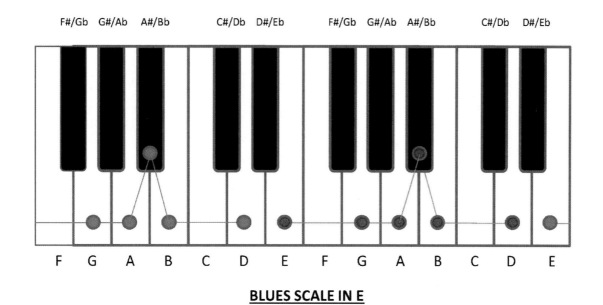

BLUES SCALE IN E

Blues Scale in Eb

$\underline{I}$	$\underline{II}$	$\underline{III}$	$\underline{IV}$	$\underline{V}$	$\underline{VI}$	$\underline{I}$
Eb	Gb	Ab	A	Bb	Db	Eb

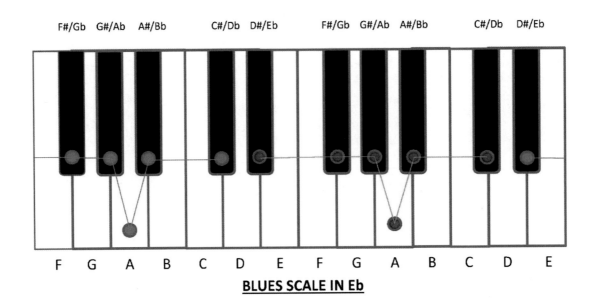

BLUES SCALE IN Eb

Blues Scale in F

<u>I</u>	<u>II</u>	<u>III</u>	<u>IV</u>	<u>V</u>	<u>VI</u>	<u>I</u>
F	Ab	Bb	B	C	Eb	F

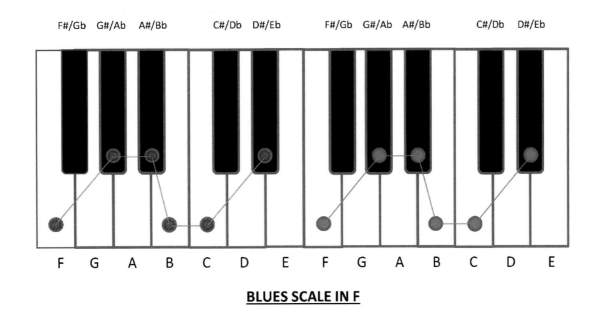

BLUES SCALE IN F

I	II	III	IV	V	VI	I
G	Bb	C	C#	D	F	G

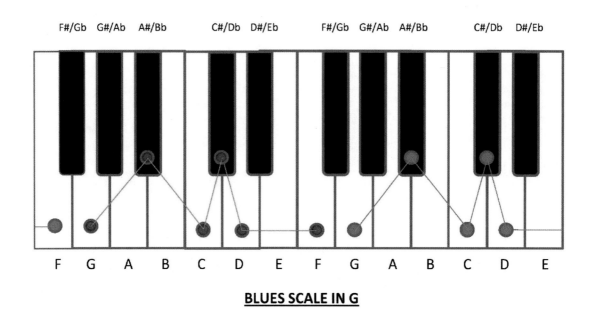

BLUES SCALE IN G

Blues Scale in Gb

I	II	III	IV	V	VI	I
Gb	A	B	C	C#	E	Gb

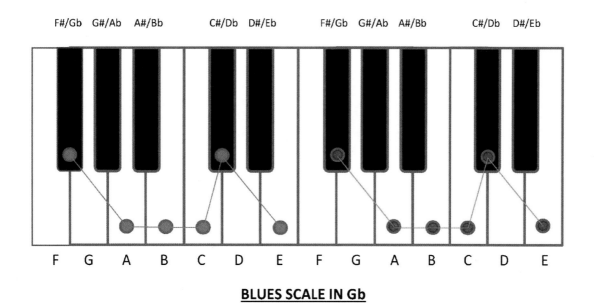

BLUES SCALE IN Gb

V. INTRODUCTION TO READING SHEET MUSIC

We can now look at the foundations of how to read music. When I say foundation, I mean exactly that. Just as a skyscraper can soar 2000 feet into the sky, it rests on, and is fastened to, a very strong and very durable foundation. Without a sturdy and dependable foundation, the skyscraper cannot stand. As you start to study music, make sure your foundations are strong. Know your scales. Understand intervals. Know the difference between major chords and minor chords. Learn your blues scales. Experiment with playing chords with your left hand, and simultaneously playing simple riffs (in the same key) with your right hand. These are all foundational skills and will serve you well as you progress on the keyboard. In this chapter we will cover the foundations of how to read music. Many people play music extremely well but cannot read music. However, being able to read music will greatly add to your ability to play new material and to help you fully develop as a musician.

Let's start with the keyboard. Each piano key plays a specific note. The name of each note will not change no matter what key you are in. For example, the Bb (B flat) key will always be a Bb key, no matter what key signature you are playing.
This sounds obvious, but some beginning students think that the notes, or keys, have different values, or different names, according to the key they are in. Thankfully, that is not the case- a C will always be a C, an A flat will always be an A flat, etc.

Let's consider the musical staff. The musical staff consists of two sections;
    1) Treble Clef—Includes all notes above middle C; Consists of five horizontal lines, four spaces, and then further divided by vertical lines which create measures, or bars.

    2) Bass Clef—Includes all notes below middle C; Consists of five horizontal lines, four spaces, and then further divided by vertical lines which create measures, or bars.

Side note: Note that <u>middle C</u> acts as a bridge between the two staffs, that is, middle C resides an equal distance from the treble staff above it and the bass staff below it. In effect, the treble staff and the bass staff "share" middle C.
Remember where middle C is located on the keyboard?
Think about that....on the keyboard, notes located within the treble clef staff are located to the right of middle C and notes written in the bass clef staff are located to the left of middle C.

TREBLE CLEF

In a very short time, you will be able to look at written sheet music and quickly identify each note.

For now, however, most people remember the notes on the <u>treble staff lines</u>

E G B D F

by the old saying, "<u>E</u>very <u>G</u>ood <u>B</u>oy <u>D</u>oes <u>F</u>ine".

For the <u>notes in the spaces</u> between the lines, remember the word

F A C E

This phrase and word only works for the treble staff. The bass staff has its own way of remembering, which we will cover in the next section.

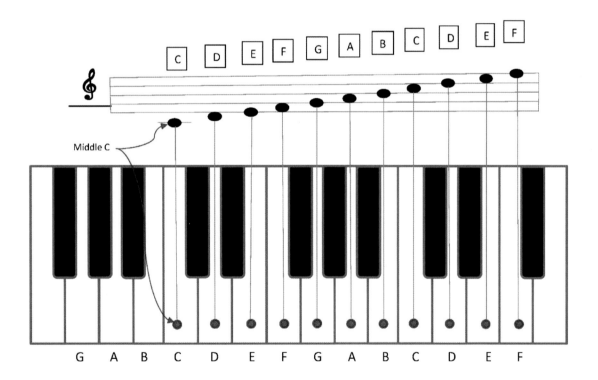

BASS CLEF

Most people remember the notes on the <u>bass staff lines</u>

G B D F A

by the quote, "<u>G</u>reat <u>B</u>ritain <u>D</u>oesn't <u>F</u>ight <u>A</u>merica".

For the <u>notes in the spaces</u> between lines

A C E G

remember the phrase, "<u>A</u>ll <u>C</u>ows <u>E</u>at <u>G</u>rass". These particular phrases only work for the bass staff. The treble staff has its own memorization tools, which we covered in the preceding section.

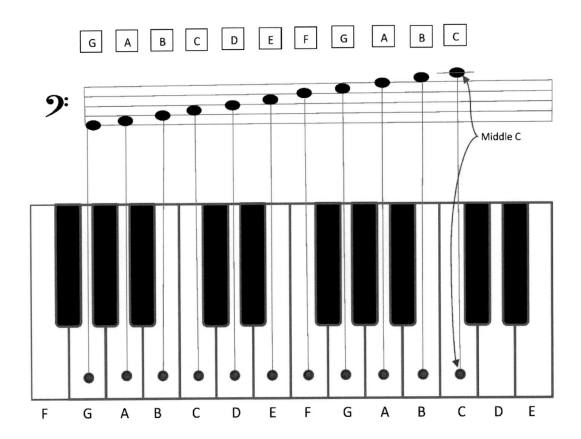

On the previous pages we made the connection between the notes as written on the sheet music and the location of those notes on the keyboard. So far, so good. But now we must discuss what is meant when we say B "flat", or D "sharp", or A "flat". What does this mean and how do we apply this knowledge?
Let's look at the keyboard again. If we want to play G, we know where G is located on both the sheet music and the keyboard.

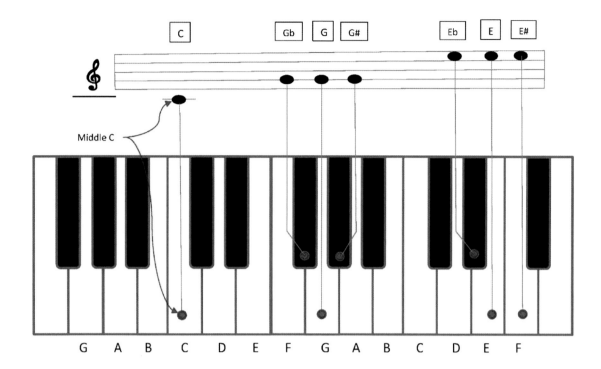

How about Gb (G flat)? When we "flatten" a note, we simply lower the note one semi-tone.

Remember that one semi-tone is the same as one half step and the same as one piano key. So, looking at the keyboard below, if we want to play Gb (G flat), we move one semi-tone to the left of G. We land on the black key. That key is G flat.

How about if we want to play G# (G sharp)? From G, we move one semi-tone to the right, and consequently land on another black key. That key is G sharp.

How do we label a "flat" or "sharp" on the written sheet music? That is a good question.

Quite simply, by placing a b in front of the note, we designate that as a flat. If we place a # in front of the note, we are designating that as a sharp.

An interesting thing happens when we want to play E# (E sharp). From E, we know we are to move one semi-tone (one half step, or one piano key) to the right. When we do this, we land on a white key. In fact, we land on what we call F. Due to the layout of the keyboard, this is correct. E# (E sharp) is, in fact, equivalent to, and equal to, F.

> **Side note:** Remember that when we sharpen a note, we raise it by one semi- tone. Some people remember this by relating it to themselves.
> If we want to look "sharp", what do we do? We raise up, stand tall, carry ourselves with confidence. When you sharpen a note, you raise it up the same way. We raise it by one semi-tone, or one piano key.
> When we flatten a note, we do the opposite; that is, we lower it by one semi-tone, or one piano key.

VI. <u>INTRODUCTION TO INTERVALS</u>

As we begin our study of piano scales and chords, we soon discover the important concept of intervals, or musical distance, between any two notes. This interval, or musical distance, determines how scales are structured, how chords are formed and ultimately how well two notes sound being played together, either sequentially (one after the other) or simultaneously (played at the same time).

To start with, let's look at how a major scale is structured.
A major scale can start on any note. We will call that starting note the tonic, or root note of the scale. We can also designate it by using a roman numeral I.

Starting with our starting note, the *tonic*, we will move up the piano keyboard using various intervals to determine which notes belong in each that scale, or key.
The distance, or interval, between notes in a major scale is based on a very specific pattern, which is;

WHOLE   WHOLE   HALF   WHOLE   WHOLE   WHOLE   HALF

What does this mean? Very simply, a <u>Whole interval</u> means 2 half steps. That makes sense, because two halves always equal one whole.
A <u>Half interval</u> means <u>one half-step.</u>
What is a half-step? **A half-step is one key on the piano**. This is also known as a semi-tone.
To illustrate, let's pull out the keyboard and examine the <u>Eb (E flat) major scale.</u>

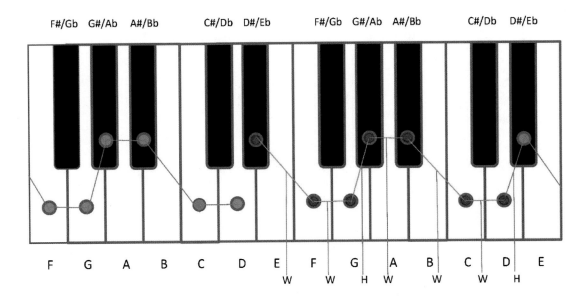

Eb Major Scale

Let's start at the root note, Eb. Remember we can call this note the *tonic*. We will also label it as roman numeral I.

The pattern, or template for major scales is this: **W W H W W W H**
Starting at Eb (our *tonic*), move one whole step (remember one whole equals two half steps, or two keys). This brings us to F. Now again, move one whole step. This brings us to G. Did you forget to count the black key? Remember, when we are counting keys, we must count both white and black keys.

Now, according to our template, we must move one half step. One half step equals one key. That brings us to G. Continuing our pattern, we will move whole (to Bb), whole (to C), whole to D, then finally half (back to Eb, our tonic). Note that when the template is followed, we end up on our *tonic*, but one octave higher.

This template, or pattern, works for every major scale. In fact, that is the definition of a major scale; that is, a major scale will start on its tonic, or root note, and following the template, identify the notes in that key and will always finish on its tonic, one octave higher.

Let's review for a second. We started on Eb, our tonic. We moved through the template and where did we land? We landed back on Eb. We landed on Eb, but one octave higher.

If we started our template again, we would hit the same notes as before, but all the notes are one octave higher. And where do we end up at the end of this template? Of course, we end up on Eb again, still another octave higher. This will occur until we run out of keys on the keyboard.

Test your understanding: Johnny "Ice Cold" Steele wanted to figure out which notes are in the key of Ab major. He started on the note Ab, and proceeded through the template of **W W H W W W H**, but he did not end up on Ab one octave higher. He claims that the pattern does not always work. What should we tell Johnny?

Let's discuss: We need to tell "Ice Cold" that the pattern does, in fact, work every time. We earlier discussed the mathematics of it; it works every single time.

He is probably not counting all the keys (black and white) or he does not understand that a Whole interval consists of two semi-tones, or two piano keys and that a Half interval consists of one semi-tone, or one piano key.

You might be asking, "What about the minor scales? How are they formed?". You are correct, the minor scales have their own unique template. We will now look at the minor scale *pattern of intervals*.

Let's examine the minor scales. How are they derived? What is the template we can use to determine the notes in a minor scale? Minor scales are derived using their own unique pattern, which is:
 WHOLE   HALF   WHOLE   WHOLE   HALF   WHOLE   WHOLE

Let's examine the **<u>Eb minor scale</u>**. We will begin on our root note, Eb. Again, we can call this our tonic, and we may even label it as roman numeral i.
The pattern, or template, for minor scales is this: **W H W W H W W**

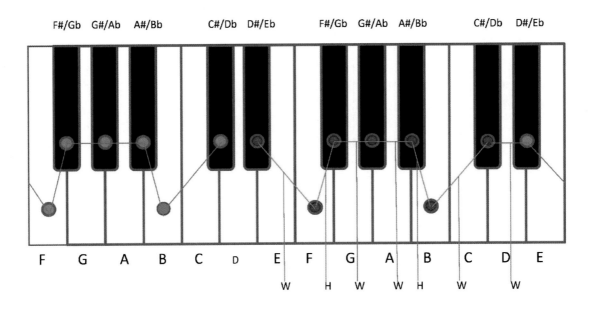

Eb minor Scale

Starting at Eb, move one whole step (to F). Now, move one half step (to Gb). Continuing the pattern for minor scales, we move whole step to Ab, whole step to Bb, half step to B, whole step to Db, then finally one whole step back to our root (one octave higher) Eb.

We have just constructed scales based on two pieces of information;

    1) The tonic, or bottom note of the scale. This gives the scale its **IDENTITY**.
        Remember we can start on any piano key we wish, black or white.
        This is the root note and will determine the **IDENTITY** of the scale.

    2) We decide whether we want to create a <u>minor scale</u> or a <u>major scale</u>.
        Starting at the root note, or tonic, a <u>minor scale</u> is created by the pattern:
        W H W W H W W.

        A <u>major scale</u> is created by starting at the root note and then using the pattern:
        W W H W W W H.
        Calling out whether a scale is a minor or major gives the scale its **QUALITY**.

When we start at the root note and then use either pattern, (either a <u>*major pattern of intervals*</u> or a <u>*minor pattern of intervals*</u>) we are identifying a "family" of notes.

We can play the notes of this family in sequence, out of sequence, up the scale, down the scale, jump around on the scale---they sound like they belong together. This family of notes is called the key.

All notes within a key are related to each other, and sound pretty good together. If you play a note which is not in the family, meaning not in that particular key, it doesn't fit, and doesn't sound right. It sounds discordant and off-key. Sometimes this is done on purpose; the band is jamming, and a discordant note is accidentally played; then on the next chorus, the discordant note is played again, with some embellishment. The next chorus, someone adds something similar. Soon, the entire jam has taken off on a creative, spontaneous journey. For now, however, let's stay with the basic structures.

Test your knowledge: We have said that all the notes within a key are related to each other? What does this mean? How are they related?

Let's discuss:
They are related musically because they are linked together by the sequence of intervals (W-W-H-W-W-W-H for major scales, and W-H-W-W-H-W-W for minor scales).

We can see that every major scale, for example, will have the same structural shape. Likewise, every minor scale is structured the same as every other minor scale.

If every major scale (or family of notes, or key) is structured similarly to every other major scale, it makes sense that each major scale would behave similarly, or would have similar characteristics to every other major scale? Wouldn't the minor scale have similar properties, similar behaviors, similar dynamics to every other minor scale?

Every W denotes two semi-tones, which is the same as two piano keys.
Every H denotes one semi-tone, or one piano key.

Both the major scale template (WWHWWWH) and the minor scale template (WHWWHWW) will mathematically add up to 12 tones, which is exactly the interval, or musical distance, of one octave.

What is an interval?
Simply put, an interval is the distance between any two notes. The distance between two notes will determine how well those two notes will combine with each other.

We describe the interval, or distance, between two notes by saying that one note is a second, or a third, or a fourth, etc. of the other. What does this mean? It really means that a note is the second, or third or fourth, etc. note on that particular scale. Remember each key has a family of notes which make up the scale. How do we know which notes are in which key?

Remember we derived the notes using
W W H W W W H to create a <u>major scale </u>and
the template **W H W W H W W** to create a <u>minor scale</u>.

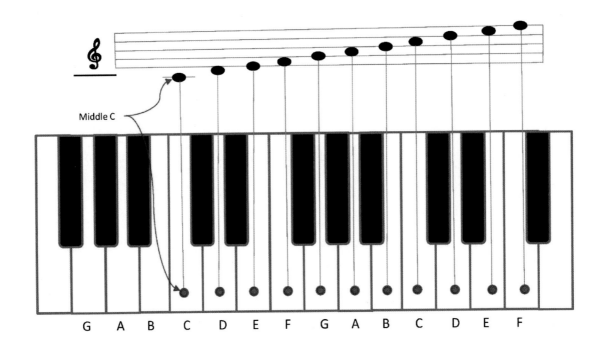

Let's look at an example. The diagram above shows the notes in the key of C major.
What is the interval between middle C and G?
We know the scale of C major is comprised of the following notes;

C D E F G A B C

We can easily see that G is the fifth note of the C major scale; hence, we can say that
in the key of C major, G is a fifth of C

However, this only tells us half the story. When we say an interval is a fifth, that
describes the <u>distance</u> between the notes. But we have to also describe the <u>quality</u> of
the interval.

But back to our example—we have looked at the notes which make up the key of C
major and have determined that G is the fifth note of the C major scale, which makes
G a fifth of C. To get the rest of the answer, we need to count the number of semi-
tones, or half notes, or piano keys that are required to reach G from C. Starting at C,
our first step is to C #, second step is to D, third step is to D #, fourth step is to E,
fifth step is to F, sixth step is to F# and seventh step is to G. This is what is known as
a perfect fifth. A <u>perfect fifth</u> has seven semi-tone "steps" between the two piano
keys in question.

Side note: A <u>perfect fifth</u> occurs when two notes are exactly seven semi-tones apart. In our major and minor scales, the fifth note will always be seven semi-tones from the tonic because we used the patterns

W W H W W W H (major keys)

and W H W W H W W to define the scales.

The fifth note of these scales will always be a perfect fifth.

That is all very convenient if we are using a scale and determining intervals from the tonic, or bottom note. What if we pick two random notes, not necessarily in the same key? How would we determine the interval in that case?

It looks complicated, but it is actually very easy. It is a two- step process, in which the first step is to determine the <u>distance</u> of the interval and the second step is to determine the <u>quality</u> of the interval.

<u>The first step</u> is to determine the <u>musical distance between the two notes in question</u>. Look at the musical staff. We already know that the staff consists of five horizontal lines, which create four spaces. Count the lines and spaces, <u>inclusive</u>, between the two notes in question.

The key word here is <u>inclusive</u>; count the line or space which the lower note is occupying and then count the lines or spaces up to, <u>and including</u>, the upper note.

<u>The second step</u> is to count the keys, or half steps, on the piano keyboard. The number of keys separating the two notes will give us the <u>quality</u> of the interval.

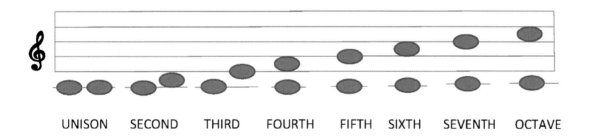

Test your understanding: Why do we need to count keys on the keyboard? Why can't we look at the staff, count the lines and spaces, inclusive, and be done with it?

Let's discuss: You may count the lines and spaces, inclusive, and you would be correct as far as determining the <u>musical distance</u>. But suppose you are looking at the interval between C and G flat. Compare that with the interval between C and G sharp. The number of the lines and spaces (inclusive, of course) will be the same, but the keyboard will yield a very different number of semi-tones between the two notes. This different number of keys would then indicate a different quality of interval. The quality of the interval can be described as perfect, diminished or augmented.

Let's try another example. What is the interval between <u>middle C</u> and <u>G flat</u>? To determine the interval, count the lines and spaces between the <u>C</u> and <u>G flat</u>. Remember that we must count the lines or spaces, and, as always, we must include the lines or spaces occupied by both the <u>C</u> and by the <u>G flat</u>.

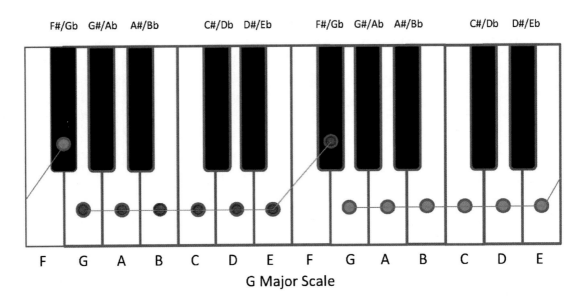

G Major Scale

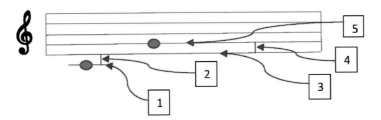

When we count the lines and spaces, we get 5. This means that G flat is a fifth of C. But remember that only tells us half the story. That tells us the distance.
 Now, getting on to the keyboard, how many semi-tones are required to move from C to G flat? Let's count these together. Starting at C, our first step is to C#, second step is to D, third step is to D sharp, fourth step is to E, fifth step is to F, sixth and final step is to G flat.

In this case we have a fifth, with six semi-tones between the two notes. This is known as a <u>diminished fifth</u>.

> **<u>Side note</u>**: When two notes are a fifth apart, and there are 7 semi-tones between them, that is known as a _perfect fifth_.

When two notes are a fifth apart, and there are 6 semi-tones between them, that is known as a *diminished fifth*.

Let's look at another example. What is the interval between A and E#?
First let's count the lines and spaces, including the spaces for A and E#.

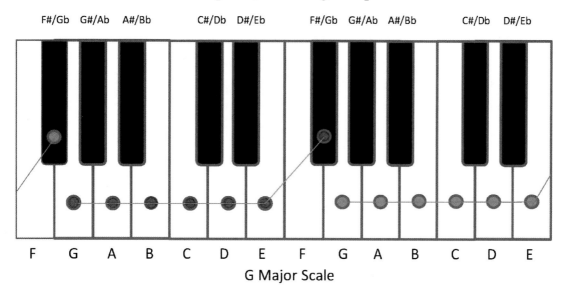

G Major Scale

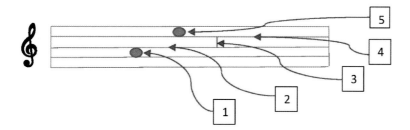

We get five bars and spaces, which tells us that A and E# are a fifth apart.
But remember, that only gives us half the story. That only tells us the <u>distance</u>.
What is the <u>quality</u> of the interval?
To answer this question we must determine how many semi-tones are required to move from A to E#. Using our keyboard, starting at A, first step is to A#, second step is to B, third step is to C, fourth step is to C#, fifth step is to D, sixth step is to D#, seventh step to to E and eighth step is to E#. In this case, we have a fifth separated by eight semi-tones. This is known as an *augmented fifth*.

<u>Side note:</u> When two notes are a fifth apart, and there are 6 semi-tones between them, that is known as a *diminished fifth*.
When two notes are a fifth apart, and there are 7 semi-tones between them, that is known as a *perfect fifth*.
When two notes are a fifth apart, and there are 8 semi-tones between them, that interval is known as an *augmented fifth*.

VII. CHORDS AND CHORD PROGRESSIONS

For our purposes, lets define a chord as a triad, that is, the sound produced when three notes are played at the same time. As we progress in our studies, we will see that chords can be made of three or more notes. Jazz, in particular, likes to use chords that can be made up of as many as 6 or 7 notes. The blues and gospel music often utilize very creative, complex and beautiful chords. For now, however, let's think of a chord in its simplest arrangement of three notes played simultaneously. We will soon discover that we cannot play, at random, just any three notes. The notes must be separated by specific _musical distances_, or what we call _intervals_. This creates _harmony_. If we should randomly pick any three notes to play together, we will very likely create _discordance_ or a _"clash"_ of sounds. We will be playing triads (three note chords) with very <u>specific intervals between the first and third note of the chord (I and III)</u>, as well as <u>very specific intervals between the third and fifth note of the chord (III and IV)</u>.

For the simplest example, lets consider a C chord played in the key of C. There are two parts to this exercise.
   1) We want to play a C chord. This means that C is the root note.
   2) We want to play in the key of C. We can refer back to our keyboard diagram.

A quick review of the notes which make up the **C scale** indicate;

I	II	**III**	IV	**V**	VI	VII	I
C	D	E	F	G	A	B	C

The three notes which would make up this <u>C chord</u> would be;
   I) C (known as the root note in this case since it is a C chord we want to play)
  III) E (because it is the third note of the scale, known as a third interval, or a third)
  V) G (because it is the fifth note of the scale, known as a fifth interval, or a fifth) We can now play the C E and G notes simultaneously. That is a C chord, a triad played with C in root position.

Root position means that the root note is played as the lowest note of the three. We will discuss _inversions_ later in this chapter. Play around with this chord; experiment with different rhythms. Play all three notes (C, E, G) simultaneously, or play them one after another. When you do that you are playing what is known as an <u>open chord</u>—same three notes but played one after another. Experiment with which sounds inspire you, move you, lead you to other sounds.

Let's try another example, this time using a slightly more difficult key. How can we play an <u>Eb minor chord</u>?

Again, there are two parts to this exercise;

      1) We want to play an Eb minor chord. This means that Eb is the root note.

      2) We want to play in the key of Eb minor. We can refer to our keyboard diagram for the <u>Eb minor scale</u>.

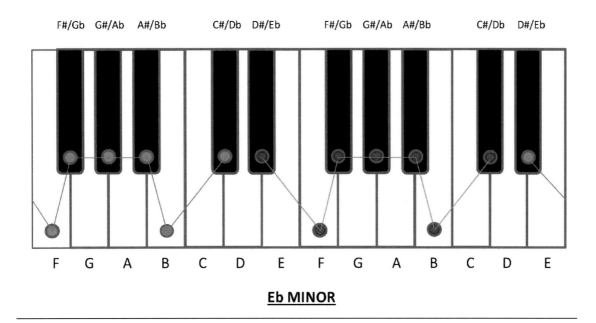

Eb MINOR

A quick review of the notes which make up the **Eb minor** scale indicate;

I	II	III	IV	V	VI	VII	I
Eb	F	**Gb**	Ab	**Bb**	B	Db	Eb

The three notes which would make up this Eb minor chord would be;

      I) Eb (known as the root note since it is an Eb minor chord we want to play)

      III) Gb (because it is the third note of the scale, known as a third interval, or a third)

      V) Bb (because it is the fifth note of the scale, known as a fifth interval, or a fifth)

Okay, let's try another one. Be patient because there is a critical lesson here that I want to show you.

We just played an **Eb minor chord**. How can we play an **Eb major chord**? What would be different? What would be the same? How can we move easily from one to the other?

There are two parts to this exercise.

      1) We want to play an Eb (major) chord. This means that Eb is the root note.

      2) We want to play in the key of Eb (major). We can refer to our keyboard diagram for the Eb major scale.

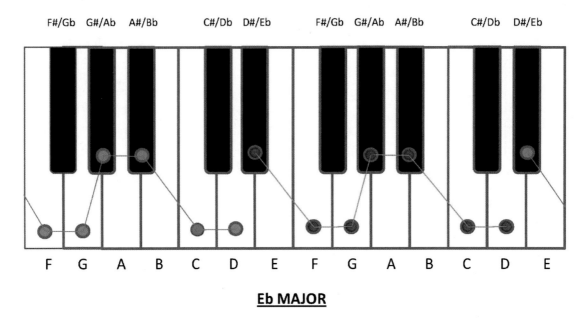

Eb MAJOR

A quick review of the notes which make up the **Eb major scale** indicate

I	ii	**iii**	IV	**V**	vi	vii	I
Eb	F	**G**	Ab	**Bb**	C	D	Eb

The three notes which would make up the <u>Eb major chord</u> would be;

    I)   Eb (again, this is the root note of the chord)

   III) G (because it is the third note of the scale, known as a third interval, or a third)

    V) Bb (because it is the fifth note of the scale, known as a fifth interval, or a fifth)

As we can see, the first note of the *Eb minor chord* and the first note of the *Eb major chord* are identical, that is, Eb. Likewise, the fifth note (V) of the *Eb minor scale* and the fifth (V) note of the *Eb major scale* are identical, that is, Bb.

The only difference is the middle note. <u>This is a critical difference</u> and the student needs to pay attention to this. As you look at a piano keyboard, become aware of the *interval,* or *musical distance*, between the I and the III in the Eb minor chord.

Playing an _Eb minor chord_, from I (Eb) to the III (Gb) there is an interval of 3 half-steps, or three piano keys. Conversely, what is the interval between I and III in the _Eb major chord_?

Playing an _Eb (major) chord_, the interval between the I (Eb) and the III (G) in the Eb major chord is 4 half steps, or 4 piano keys.

Let's stop for a moment and contemplate this. What we have just discovered will give you an intimate understanding of how to construct a minor chord, a major chord and will give you the ability to change between the two.

Let that sink in for a minute.

A) A major chord has 4 semi-tones between the first and middle note.
    A minor chord has 3 semi-tones between the first and middle note.
    First (I) and third (V) notes of the chord remain the same.

B) We have already agreed that since each major scale is constructed similarly to every other major chord, this rule applies to all scales and all keys.

C) Likewise, we have agreed that since all minor scales are constructed in the same way as every other minor scale, this rule applies to all minor scales.

Meditate on this idea and visualize playing every chord as major or minor; the musical distance, or _interval_, between the first note and middle note of a chord determines whether that chord is a minor chord (with three half-steps) or a major chord (with four half-steps). The first and third notes are the same, with only the middle note being different. This is a critical and useful concept. After a little practice, you will be able to easily change back and forth between major and minor chords in any key.

Test Your Understanding: Kit Kat "Little Miss Trouble" Treble knows that playing the notes **D F A** creates a **D minor chord**. Her bandmates ask her if it is possible to quickly change to a **D major chord** and then back again to **D minor chord**.

Let's discuss: Kit tells them that they still play the D and A notes (I and V), but that they need to increase the interval between I and III (the first and middle notes) So instead of playing **D F A**, they must "sharpen" the **F** (middle note) to F# (thereby increasing the interval by one semi-tone) and will then play **D F# A** to create a **D major chord**.

To return to D minor chord, go back to **D F A.**

Going one step further

Up until now, we have been focusing on playing chords based on the root note. We played a C chord in the key of C. We played an Eb minor chord and an Eb major chord in the key of Eb.

Let's take it one step further now. Let's go back to the key of C.
Again, a quick review of the notes which make up the C scale indicate;

I	ii	iii	IV	V	vi	vii	I
C	D	E	F	G	A	B	C

Now, instead of playing a root chord (consisting of notes I, III and V or C, E and G), lets play a different chord in the key of C. Let's start on III, which is the note E. We will now play notes III, V and VII (three, five, seven) or E, G and B. This creates an **E minor chord.**

> **Side Note**: Remember what we discovered about the interval between the first and middle notes in both major and minor chords?
> When we play the notes E G B that is an E minor chord.
> It is an E chord because E is the root note.
> It is a minor chord because the interval between the first and middle notes (between E and G) is three semi-tones.

We don't need to stop there. Staying in the key of C, we can start on IV, which is the note F. We would then play IV, VI and I (four, six and eight, which is I). This creates an **F major chord.**

I	ii	iii	IV	V	vi	vii	I
C	D	E	F	G	A	B	C

Why did we create a minor chord when starting on iii (E) and a major chord when starting on IV (F)?
Let's go back to what we learned about the interval, or distance, between the first note of the chord and the second note of the chord. An interval of 3 half tones (3 piano keys) between the first and second notes in a triad chord creates a minor chord; an interval of 4 half tones (4 piano keys) creates a major chord. This creates the very distinct difference in sound between a major chord and a minor chord. Major chords tend to sound bright, happy, and peaceful. Minor chords tend to sound more emotional, sometimes poignant, sometimes mysterious, sad or even scary.

Experiment for yourself. Pick any key and become familiar with the scale. Bear in mind that <u>the notes of the scale now become your building blocks for constructing chords</u>. Some chords sound "natural", "stable", "centered"; others tend to sound incomplete, as if they want to lead you to another chord, and that chord may sound like it wants to lead you back to the original chord. In other words, certain chords sound perfectly matched with other chords when played in sequence. Two, three or more chords can be played in a certain order, and they sound good together. They sometimes create a certain tension, or expectation, and then they finally reach resolution, or completion when the final chord is played. This process of creating tension and expectation and then resolving it, is one of the basic ideas behind chord progression.

Let's play something to illustrate this whole idea of chord progression. Let's turn to the key of **G major.**

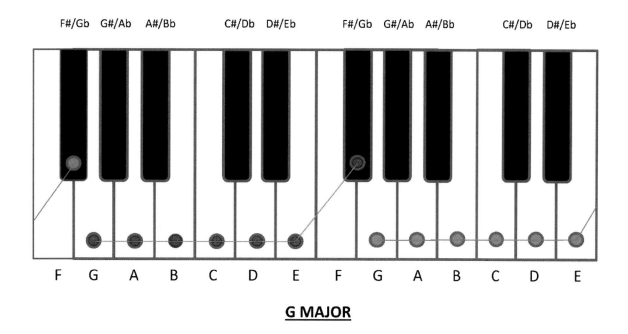

G MAJOR

A quick review of the notes which make up the **G major** scale indicate:

I	ii	iii	IV	V	vi	vii	I
G	A	B	C	D	E	F#	G

Below is a table summarizing the basic chords that can be constructed in the key of G.

Degree	Chord	Notes		
I:	G	G	B	D
ii:	Am	A	C	E
iii:	Bm	B	D	F#
IV:	C	C	E	G
V:	D	D	F#	A
vi:	Em	E	G	B
vii:	F# dim	F#	A	C

Side note: Did you notice that the first, fourth and fifth degree chords are all major chords? That is why the roman numerals are all capitals while the others chords are minor chords, designated by lower case roman numerals. This pattern is typical when playing in a major key. The one exception (in major keys) is the vii chord. It is a diminished chord. We will discuss *diminished chords* and *augmented chords* in detail later in the book.

Let's play a very popular chord progression known as a I-IV-V or "1-4-5".

A) Start out by playing the **I chord** (G major) made up of the G B D notes.
   Play around with that chord, try different rhythms, different tempos....
B) Then play the **IV chord** (C major) made up of C E G notes.
   Again, experiment with different tempos....
C) Play the **I chord**, followed by the **IV chord**.
   Play a riff that sounds good to you, vary the tempo, play something that sounds cool to you...
   Can you feel how some tension is created, as if the sequence is incomplete?
   Can you hear how the sequence wants to resolve itself, wants to "complete" the tension?
D) Now, play the **V chord** (D major) made up of D F# A notes.
   This brings the whole chord progression together and seems to complete the sequence, to resolve the sequence, to complete the chord progression.

Congratulations, you have just played your first Chord Progression!
You will soon discover that chord progressions form the backbone of literally hundreds, if not thousands of popular songs. More about that later.

Let's try another example. Here is another very popular progression known as a "2-5-1" or "ii-v-I".

For this exercise, let's play in the key of **Eb minor**.

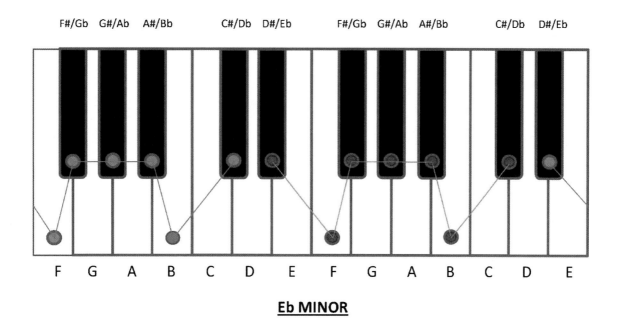

Eb MINOR

A quick review of the notes which make up the Eb minor scale indicate:

i	ii	III	iv	v	VI	VII	i
Eb	F	Gb	Ab	Bb	B	Db	Eb

Constructing a table showing the basic chords in the key of Eb minor;

Degree	Chord	Notes		
i:	Ebm	Eb	Gb	Bb
ii:	F dim	F	Ab	B
III:	Gb	Gb	Bb	Db
iv:	Abm	Ab	B	Eb
v:	Bbm	Bb	Db	F
VI:	B	B	Eb	Gb
VII:	Db	Db	F	Ab

Side note: Did you notice that the third, sixth, and seventh degree chords are all major chords? That is why III, VI and VII are upper case roman numerals. The other chords are minor chords, designated by lower case roman numerals. This pattern is typical when playing in a minor key. The one exception (in minor keys) is the ii chord; it is a *diminished* chord. We will discuss *diminished chords* and *augmented* chords in detail later in this book.

A) Start out by playing the **ii chord** (F dim) made up of the **F Ab B** notes.
   Play around with that chord, try different rhythms, different tempos....
B) Then play the **v chord** (Bb minor) made up of **Bb Db F** notes.
C) Play the **ii chord**, followed by the **v chord**.
   Again, experiment with different tempos and different rhythms.....
   Can you hear how tension is created, as if the sequence is incomplete?
   Can you hear how the sequence wants to resolve itself?
D) Now, play the **i chord** (Eb minor) made up of **Eb Gb Bb** notes.
   This brings the whole chord progression together and brings resolution, or completeness, to the chord progression.

Inverted Chords

Earlier in this section on Chords and Chord Progressions, we agreed to construct our chords as a triad, using three notes. This is the simplest type of chord. Later in your playing, you will start to use chords made up of 4, 5 or more notes. Jazz calls upon many complex and interesting chords and voicings.

Remember the <u>C chord</u>? It is made up of the notes **C E G**. The note C is the root note, and as such, is the lowest note of the three notes which make up the chord.

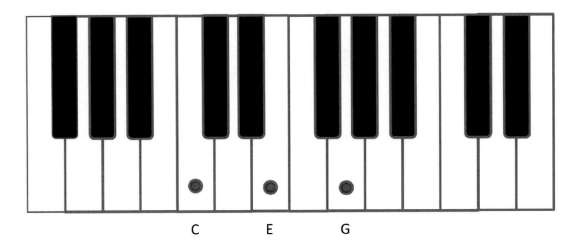

What would happen if we played the notes C, E and G but in a different order?

Let's play the notes C E G, but let's play the C note one octave higher. In effect we are playing **E G C**. This is known as a *C chord, first inversion.* We have taken the root note (C) and instead of making it the lowest note in the chord, we are playing the C note one octave higher. This voicing is still a C chord, but known as an inverted chord, in this case, the *first inversion.*

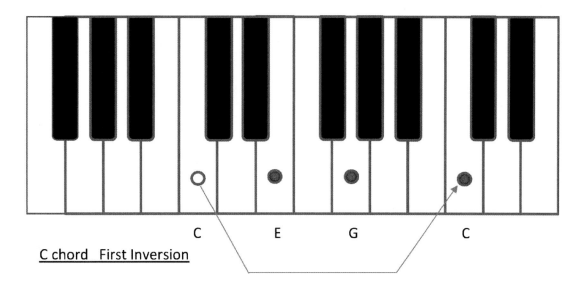

C chord   First Inversion

Now let's change the order again. Let's move the note E up one octave. In effect we are now playing **G   C E**. This is called *C chord, second inversion.* Here we are playing both C and E one octave higher, while the G remains in original position. Again, it is a C chord, but known as the *second inversion.*

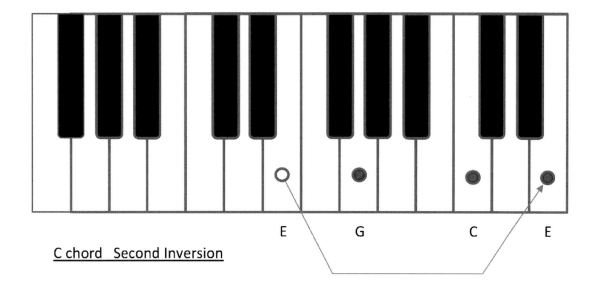

C chord   Second Inversion

What would happen if we now move the G note to the higher octave? Now, we are back to playing a C chord in root position, but the entire chord is now one octave higher. Why would we do this? Why would we take a perfectly great sounding chord and change the order?

The main reason to change the order of a chord, that is, to play an inversion of that chord, is often to add interest to a chord progression.

For example, suppose you wanted to play a i-iv-v chord progression in the key of A minor.

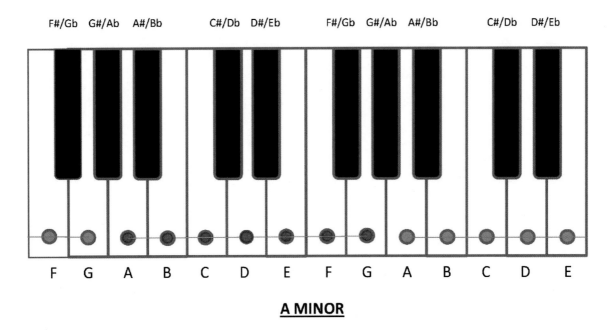

A MINOR

To play a i-iv-v, we could play it straight, that is, as below;
    A minor: A C E
    D minor: D F A
    E minor: E G B
If we play the progression like this, there is nothing wrong with that. However, the sound could sound a little abrupt, a little disconnected.

As an alternative, we could play it as follows;
    A minor: <u>A C E</u>
    D minor (second inversion): <u>A   D F</u> (both D and F have moved up)
    E minor (first inversion): <u>G B E</u>   (E has moved up)

Instead of moving around, all over the keyboard, we can arrange our progressions so that there is a minimum of distance between following chords. Sure, at times you may want a drastic sounding difference to accentuate, etc. but at other times you may like the ease of playing, plus the added interest of different sounds with more complex, inverted chord progressions.

VIII. INTRODUCTION TO 12 BAR BLUES

Now that we have been introduced to the whole idea of chord progressions, that is, playing certain chords in a certain sequence which creates harmony, tension, interest and finally resolution, we want to take this idea to the next level.

We have heard the dynamics, the tension and the resolution of playing a I-IV-V (1-4-5) progression in any major key.   Let's review a I-IV-V chord progression in the key of C.

> Side Note: As we discussed earlier in the book, we will refer to major keys as only B or C or Eb or G or whatever. We understand that when we see B or Eb or G, (with no modifier) that indicates that it is a <u>major</u> key (or chord). Only when a key (or chord) is minor, only then will we add a modifier.

A quick review of the notes which make up the key of C indicate:

<u>I</u>	<u>ii</u>	<u>iii</u>	<u>IV</u>	<u>V</u>	<u>vi</u>	<u>vii</u>	<u>I</u>
C	D	E	F	G	A	B	C

<u>Degree</u>	<u>Chord</u>	<u>Notes</u>		
I:	C	C	E	G
IV:	F	F	A	C
V:	G	G	B	D

We learned that we can play the I-IV-V sequence and it sounds good. But let's take it another step.

Let's play the following chords.   Hold each chord for 4 beats, then go to the next chord. Play the 4 chords on the top row (each chord for 4 beats, a total of 16 beats), then play the middle row (again, 4 beats x 4 chords =16 beats), and then the bottom row (same 4 x 4 beats as before)

Bar 1 I	Bar 2 I	Bar 3 I	Bar 4 I		Bar 1 C	Bar 2 C	Bar 3 C	Bar 4 C
Bar 5 IV	Bar 6 IV	Bar 7 I	Bar 8 I	**or**	Bar 5 F	Bar 6 F	Bar 7 C	Bar 8 C
Bar 9 V	Bar 10 IV	Bar 11 I	Bar 12 I		Bar 9 G	Bar 10 F	Bar 11 C	Bar 12 C

Each I or C indicates C chord (C E G)
Each V or G indicates G chord (G B D)
Each IV or F indicates F chord (F A C)
Each chord played for four beats, then move to next chord

Congratulations, you have just played your first 12 bar blues! You played 12 bars, with each bar consisting of a chord being held for four beats. In this case, 4 beats equal one bar, or one measure. You might be asking, "How fast should my beats be? Should I be going faster or slower?" Hey, you are the musician.... you can decide which sounds right for you. You might want a slow, soulful number or you may want to rock out, or anything in between.

Here is a variation. We will still play 12 bars. Each bar will still consist of 4 beats. But, instead of holding each chord for four beats, you play each chord for one beat, four times per measure. That approach would look like this:

Bar 1 CCCC   Bar 2 CCCC   Bar 3 CCCC   Bar 4 CCCC

Bar 5 FFFF   Bar 6 FFFF   Bar 7 CCCC   Bar 8 CCCC

Bar 9 GGGG   Bar 10 FFFF   Bar 11 CCCC   Bar 12 CCCC

Remember to play the four bars across the top, then the middle row, then the bottom row (total of 12 bars; each bar has 4 beats)

Each C indicates C chord (C E G)
Each G indicates G chord (G B D)
Each F indicates F chord (F A C)

After you play this arrangement a few times, you can add a little interest by mixing up the rhythm a little bit.
For example, in the third bar, instead of a steady rhythm, you can add a quick half step, or start playing the third bar perhaps one half beat ahead of the rhythm and then hold the note to get back into rhythm. You will soon start adding your own twists and turns to make it more and more interesting.

Another way to add interest is to slightly modify what you are playing in the final (12th) bar. In the final bar, instead of playing CCCC you can play CCGG or something similar. This sets up a transition going back to the first bar.

Let's do a quick review. We learned about chords, and for the time being, we agreed to play chords as a triad, or chords made up of three notes. We know that we can invert chords by playing the same three notes but in a different order. Then we played different chords in sequence, which we called chord progressions. The chord progressions were harmonious, often creating a musical tension, and then were resolved.
Finally, we played chord progressions in a 12-bar structure, which is a framework which uses this tension and resolution to create a background for many popular songs. As you play a 12-bar blues, which is a framework for a song, other instruments in the band may play their own riff or solo. In this case, you, as the

keyboardist, may be keeping the beat, along with the bass and drummer, keeping the framework intact. Other times, the guitar, for instance, may be playing a 12-bar rhythm and you, the keyboardist, may be carrying the melody, playing your own solo or adding your own riffs.

TAKING IT TO THE NEXT LEVEL

I want to introduce you to a new type of chord. For starters, it is made up of four notes. We have been playing triads for the most part, but here we are adding a 7th (seventh). To add this note, add a minor third (three semi-tones) to the third note of your chord.

Changing a C chord to C dominant 7th chord

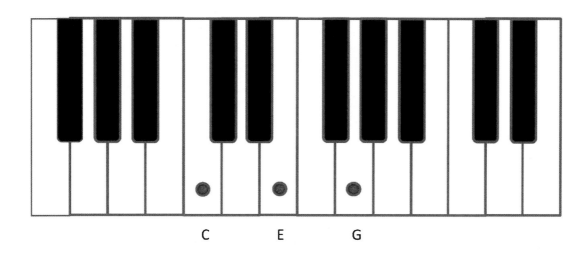

C chord, with C in the root position

Here is a C chord, a triad, made of 3 notes.

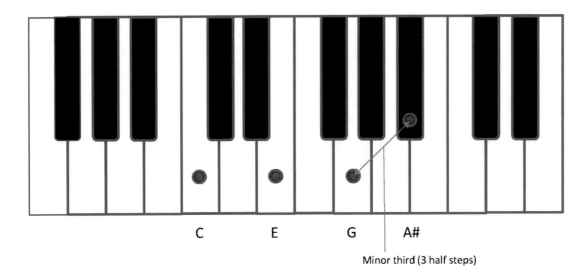

C7 chord, with C in the root position

And here is the <u>C7 chord</u> with C in the root position. Note that <u>we have added a minor third (3 half notes) to the existing C chord.</u> A minor third (3 half steps) above the note G brings us to A#.

These four notes create a C7 chord, known as a *C dominant 7th chord*.

Changing an F chord to F dominant 7th chord

Below is an F chord, in root position, one of the many triad chords we have been playing.

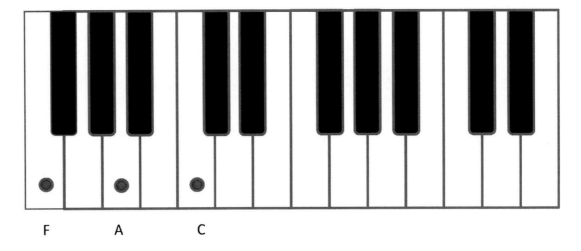

F chord, with F in the root position

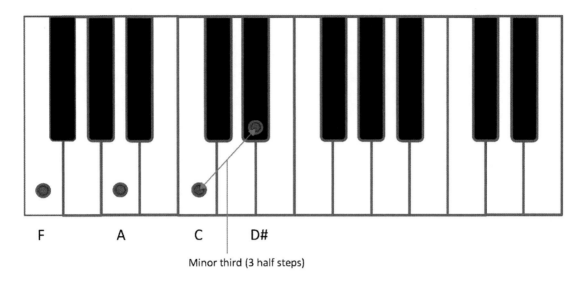

F | A | C | D#

Minor third (3 half steps)

F7 chord, with F in the root position

And here is the <u>F7 chord</u> with F in the root position. Note that <u>we have added a minor third (3 half notes) to the existing F chord</u>. A minor third (3 half steps) above the note C brings us to D#. These four notes create a F7 chord, known as a *F dominant 7th chord*.

Changing a G chord to G dominant 7th chord

Below is a G chord, with G in root position. Just like we did with the C and F chords above, we are going to add a fourth note to the existing G chord. We will add this fourth note three semi-tones above the existing top note of the chord.

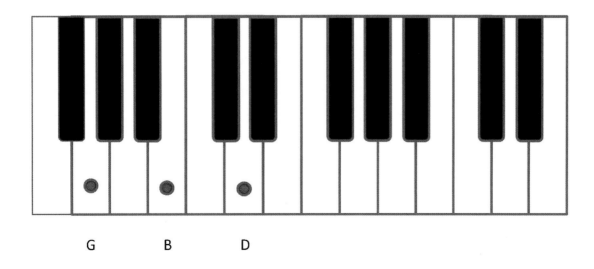

G | B | D

G chord, with G in the root position

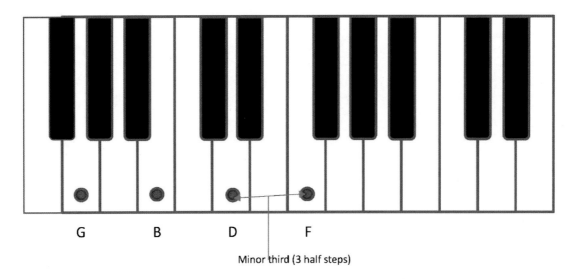

G7 chord, with G in the root position

And here is the <u>G7 chord</u> with G in the root position. Note that <u>we have added a minor third (3 half notes) to the existing G chord</u>. A minor third (3 half steps) above the note D brings us to F.

This creates a G7 chord, known as a *G dominant 7ᵗʰ chord*.

You have just been introduced to one of the most beautiful, useful, versatile and thrilling parts of playing music on a piano. Everybody loves the sound of a chord made up of three notes-what we called a triad. By inverting a three note chord, using them in progressions, using them as a rhythm, they are truly beautiful. But you have just played a chord with four notes. You will see that chords made of four, five or six notes can sound exhilarating and are always played with emotion.

But let's stay on track here. There will be plenty of time for you to experiment with all types of complex chord structures. For now, I want to apply these new chords (C7, F7 and G7) to the 12-bar blues.

Let's play a I-IV-V in the key of C7. We did this before, but this time let's use what is known as a dominant 7ᵗʰ chord.

Remember to play the top row, then middle, then bottom row

I	I	I	I		C7	C7	C7	C7	Each I or C7 indicates C7 chord (C E G A#)
IV	IV	I	I	<u>OR</u>	F7	F7	C7	C7	Each IV or F7 indicates F7 chord (F A C D#)
V	IV	I	I		G7	F7	C7	C7	Each V or G7 indicates G7 chord (G B D F)

Each chord played and held for four beats, or for a different sound, instead of holding each chord for four beats, you can play each chord for one beat, four times per measure. You decide what tempo you like.

C7 C7 C7 C7	C7 C7 C7 C7	C7 C7 C7 C7	C7 C7 C7 C7
F7 F7 F7 F7	F7 F7 F7 F7	C7 C7 C7 C7	C7 C7 C7 C7
G7 G7 G7 G7	F7 F7 F7 F7	C7 C7 C7 C7	C7 C7 C7 C7

Each C7 indicates C7 chord (C E G A#)
Each F7 indicates F7 chord (F A C D#)
Each G7 indicates G7 chord (G B D F)
Each chord played for one beat

12 Bar Blues Reference Charts

By now you have a pretty good feel for how the 12 bar blues can be constructed, how they can be modified, stretched and improvised upon. The following charts may be useful to you as you practice the 12 bar structure in various keys. You will notice that all the chords are major keys with dominant 7th.
Let's not get overwhelmed here.
   a) It's a major chord, which means 4 semi-tones between first and second note.
   b) It contains a perfect fifth (seven semi-tones) between first and third notes.
   c) It is a dominant 7th, so we have added a minor third (three semi-tones) at the top end.

Rome wasn't built in a day, so this will take some time to master. Have fun with it, stretch it and bend it and find the sound you like.

12 bar blues in A Major

A7	A7	A7	A7		A7:	A	C#	E	G
D7	D7	A7	A7		D7:	D	F#	A	C
E7	D7	A7	E7		E7:	E	G#	B	D

12 bar blues in Ab Major

Ab7	Ab7	Ab7	Ab7		Ab7:	Ab	C	Eb	Gb
Db7	Db7	Ab7	Ab7		Db7:	Db	F	Ab	B
Eb7	Db7	Ab7	Eb7		Eb7:	Eb	G	Bb	C#

12 bar blues in B Major

B7	B7	B7	B7
Eb7	Eb7	B7	B7
F#7	Eb7	B7	F#7

B7:   B   Eb   F#   A
Eb7:   Eb   G   Bb   C#
F#7:   F#   Bb   C#   E

12 bar blues in Bb Major

Bb7	Bb7	Bb7	Bb7
Eb7	Eb7	Bb7	Bb7
F7	Eb7	Bb7	F7

Bb7:   Bb   D   Ab
Eb7:   Eb   G   Bb   Db
F7:   F   A   C   Eb

12 bar blues in C

C7	F7	C7	C7
F7	F7	C7	A7
Dm7	G7	Em7	Dm7/G7

C7:   C   E   G   Bb
F7:   F   A   C   Eb
A7:   A   C#   E   G
Dm7:   D   F   A   C
Em7:   E   G   B   D
G7:   G   B   D   F

12 bar blues in D

D7	D7	D7	D7
G7	G7	D7	D7
A7	G7	D7	D7

D7:   D   F#   A   C
G7:   G   B   D   F
A7:   A   C#   E   G

12 bar blues in Db Major

Db7	Db7	Db7	Db7
Gb7	Gb7	Db7	Db7
Ab7	Gb7	Db7	Ab7

Db7:   Db   F   G#   B
Gb7:   Gb   A#   Db   E
Ab7:   Ab   C   D#   Gb

12 bar blues in E Major

E7	E7	E7	E7
A7	A7	E7	E7
B7	A7	E7	B7

E7:   E   G#   B   D
A7:   A   C#   E   G
B7:   B   D#   F#   A

12 bar blues in Eb Major

Eb7	Eb7	Eb7	Eb7		Eb7:	Eb	G	Bb	Db
Ab7	Ab7	Eb7	Eb7		Ab7:	Ab	C	Eb	Gb
Bb7	Ab7	Eb7	Bb7		Bb7:	Bb	D	F	Ab

12 bar blues in F Major

F7	F7	F7	F7		F7:	F	A	C	Eb
Bb7	Bb7	F7	F7		Bb7:	Bb	D	F	Ab
C7	Bb7	F7	C7		C7:	C	E	G	Bb

12 bar blues in G Major

G7	G7	G7	G7		G7:	G	B	D	F
C7	C7	G7	G7		C7:	C	E	G	Bb
D7	C7	G7	D7		D7:	D	F#	A	C

12 bar blues in Gb Major

Gb7	Gb7	Gb7	Gb7		Gb7:	Gb	A#	Db	E
B7	B7	Gb7	Gb7		B7:	B	D#	F#	A
Db7	B7	Gb7	Gb7		Db7:	Db	F	G#	B

ONE FINAL EXERCISE

Okay, we have covered a lot of material in this book from basic keyboard layout to an introduction to the 12 bar blues. However, I want to leave you with one final exercise, one final blues riff to practice. It is a 12-bar blues riff, with one or two slight twists that I think you will like.

We will be playing in the key of C, which lends itself well to this exercise.

1) CG CG CA CA   **2)** CG CG CA CA   **3)** CG CG CA CA   **4)** CG CG CA CA

5) FC FC FD FD   **6)** FC FC FD FD   **7)** CG CG CA CA   **8)** CG CG CA CA

9) GD GD GE GE   **10)** FC FC FD FD   **11)** CG CG CA CA   **12)** CG CG CA CA

Instead of playing full chords, we will play partial chords, or voicings. For example, in Bar 1 we will play the C and G together, again C and G together, then C and A together, and again C and A together. Each voicing will be for one beat. Then, on to Bar 2, each pairing, or voicing for one beat. You will soon find, however, that a steady beat will soon be replaced with a bluesy shuffle type beat. What I mean is, that instead of a 1-2-3-4 type steady beat, think more of a 1 and 2 and 1 and 2 type of slightly off-beat rhythm. You can improvise and accentuate that bluesy beat all you want.

Now, in your right hand.....go up one octave and find C. Go up another octave to the next C. With your right hand (thumb and pinkie, or thumb and fourth finger) play the two C's together, in rhythm with what you are playing with your left hand.

One final word

You have now started on your musical journey. You will undoubtedly hit a few plateaus on your journey. At times, it may seem like you are not making progress for maybe a week or more. Then suddenly things fall into place. Do not get discouraged when you hit those plateaus. I know many very accomplished musicians and they all tell me they have experienced these temporary plateaus and they always work themselves out.

Also, you may be telling yourself, "What's the use? I will be "x" years old by the time I am any good." First of all, you can derive much joy from learning and you can enjoy the journey right now. Secondly, believe it or not, someday you will be "x" years old anyway. At that point you may wish you had stayed with it and developed such a beautiful talent.

Good luck to all of you. I hope this book will help you to move forward in your musical journey and I hope it will provide information and inspiration for you and yours. Best wishes, good luck and see you down the road.......

Made in the USA
Coppell, TX
08 November 2020